PIRATES IN THE
AGE OF SAIL

A NORTON CASEBOOK IN HISTORY

Robert J.

this book is
for my daughter
Karen

W. W. Norton & Company has been independent since its founding in 1923, when William Warder Norton and Mary D. Herter Norton first published lectures delivered at the People's Institute, the adult education division of New York City's Cooper Union. The Nortons soon expanded their program beyond the Institute, publishing books by celebrated academics from America and abroad. By mid-century, the two major pillars of Norton's publishing program—trade books and college texts—were firmly established. In the 1950s, the Norton family transferred control of the company to its employees, and today—with a staff of four hundred and a comparable number of trade, college, and professional titles published each year—W. W. Norton & Company stands as the largest and oldest publishing house owned wholly by its employees.

Printed in the United States of America.

The text of this book is composed in Baskerville MT with the display set in Cloister Openface.

Composition by ElectraGraphics, Inc.

Series design by Jo Anne Metsch.

Manufacturing by Courier, Westford.

Project editor: Lory Frenkel.

Production manager: Benjamin Reynolds.

Library of Congress Cataloging-in-Publication Data

Antony, Robert J.
    Pirates in the age of sail : a Norton casebook / Robert J. Antony.
       p. cm.
    ISBN-13: 978-0-393-92788-7 (pbk.)
    ISBN-10: 0-393-92788-1 (pbk.)

    1. Pirates—History. I. Title.

    G535.A584 2007
    910.4'5—dc22

                                                                        2006048085

W. W. Norton & Company, Inc., 500 Fifth Avenue, New York, N.Y. 10110-0017
www.wwnorton.com
W. W. Norton & Company Ltd., Castle House, 75/76 Wells Street, London W1T 3QT

1 2 3 4 5 6 7 8 9 0

CONTENTS

iii

LIST OF FIGURES, TABLES, AND MAPS

ACKNOWLEDGMENTS

I am grateful to many colleagues, students, and friends who have helped in one way or another in the writing of this book—Lanshin Chang, Marcus Dukes, Stefan Eklöf, Huang Guosheng, Ikuya Tokoro, Selina Langford, Emily Moore, Ota Atsushi, Michael Pearson, Bill Porter, Philip Shaw, Jim Warren, and Zheng Guangnan. Thanks also are due to the researchers, archivists, and librarians at the Quanzhou Maritime History Museum (China), University of Hawaii's Hamilton Library, Huntington Library (San Marino), New York Public Library, Peabody Essex Museum (Salem), Netherlands Maritime Museum (Amsterdam), University of Oklahoma's Bizzell Memorial Library, Shantou Municipal Library (China), Port Townsend Public Library (Washington), Vancouver Maritime Museum, Western Kentucky University Library, First Historical Archives (Beijing), and Academia Sinica's Fu Sinian Library (Taiwan). Much of the research for this book, which took me to several continents, was funded by grants from the Fulbright Foundation and Western Kentucky University, for which I am indebted.

I
Overview

Introduction

"Pirate Killings Worldwide Increasing," the headline read. Conjuring up visions of bloodthirsty, swashbuckling pirates, this caption could have been taken from a seventeenth-century London broadside, but it actually comes from an International Maritime Bureau report dated 1999. After a hiatus during the late nineteenth and early twentieth centuries, piracy is once again on the rise worldwide. Many of the areas where piracy prevails today are also areas where it thrived two and three centuries ago. Likewise, many of the reasons for piracy today are the same as in the past. Ships of economically advanced nations have always followed sea routes that have taken them past some of the poorest and most underdeveloped areas of the world. Prosperity and poverty have always gone hand in hand with surges in piracy. Visible wealth, in the form of large amounts of goods and money being transported by ship, provides greater opportunities and temptations for people to commit crime, especially for those living in less developed areas. As in former times, today's pirates often operate in collusion with officials who give them protection for money. The current resurgence in piracy invites us to examine the problem from the vantage point of history.

Pirates are intrinsically interesting. Over the centuries, piracy has continued to capture the imaginations of writers and readers alike. Whether described as daring adventurers, heroic rebels, or murderous villains, pirates in fact and fiction continue to fascinate people of all ages. Although the golden age of piracy ended over a hundred years ago, nevertheless our fascination continues to the present. Novels, cartoons, and movies about pirates are more popular today than ever before. Surfing the World Wide Web one can easily find hundreds of sites filled with images of pirate flags, buried treasures, and weapons, as well as biographies of infamous pirates of the past. Pirates have remained so interesting perhaps because, at least in the popular imagination, they have been depicted as both ruthless villains and romantic heroes.

Nonetheless, we should study piracy not simply because it is interesting but also because it is important. Pirates played a significant role in the development of early modern society, culture, and history. This book takes a global perspective to explore the world of pirates between the early sixteenth and middle nineteenth centuries. It examines major events and personalities in the history of piracy. The approach, what historians call "history from below," allows readers to examine pirates on their own terms and to reconstruct their daily lives and aspirations. We will look at key historical issues concerning political, social, and economic transformations, cultural and religious diversity, and gender and sexuality. The book is divided into three sections: one, historical overview, two, historical documents and case studies, and three, recent interpretative essays.

The overview section provides a historical synopsis of piracy around the world in the age of sail, as well as introducing key analytical problems addressed in the documents and interpretative essays that follow. This section presents a narrative history of Western pirates, Mediterranean corsairs, Chinese pirates, Southeast Asian sea raiders, and contemporary pirates. The following discussions pay close attention to how we define piracy in its global and historical contexts. Although everyone seems to know what pirates are supposed to look like, they are not so easy to define. There is a plethora of terms used for pirates: privateersmen, buccaneers, corsairs, freebooters, ladrones, sea dogs, wakō, dayaks, commerce raiders, and more. It should be obvious, therefore, that we need to view piracy not as a static but as a fluid, malleable concept with complex layers of meaning relative to time, place, and culture.

Because piracy was not limited to the Western world, it is important that we take a global perspective. Today, as in the past, the highest number of piracies is in Asian waters. During the sixteenth and seventeenth centuries, Asia was at the far end of a "great pirate belt" that stretched all the way from the Caribbean to the South China Sea. At the height of piracy in the West in the early eighteenth century the total number of pirates never exceeded 5,500 men at any one time, but in China during its heyday at the start of the nineteenth century there were no fewer than 70,000 pirates. Piracy was, and still is, a worldwide phenomenon and therefore must be studied in its global context. Table 1 provides a comparative chronology of worldwide piracy in the age of sail.

The pirate ship—like other ships—was a world in miniature. Aboard sailing vessels one could find men, women, and children of diverse social, cultural, ethnic, and national backgrounds. Pirate crews were a motley assortment, not merely of rogues and social misfits, but also of ordinary sailors and fishermen who routinely alternated between licit and illicit pursuits in making a living. Besides exploring these issues, we will also explore hotly contested questions concerning pirate utopias, sexuality, and gender relations. Did pirates form a democratic and egalitarian social order that created "a world turned upside down"? Did female pirates enjoy the same rights and rewards as did their male counterparts? These questions have usually been framed simply within the context of Western piracy, but did Asian and other non-Western pirates behave and believe as did Western pirates? This casebook provides a set of documents which allows readers to examine for themselves the issues raised in the historical narrative and in the concluding interpretative essays.

This book also examines the important role that piracy, in its multiple dimensions and definitions, played in shaping early modern history. For example, in an age of empire building and intense commercial rivalry, newly emerging or weak states supported piracy (often under the guise of privateering) as a means of expanding and consolidating their political power and economic base. In Barbary the revenues derived from corsairing were essential to the state treasury and corsair captains were key members of

Years	Western Pirates	Barbary Corsairs	China Pirates	Southeast Asian Raiders
1500		Aruj Barbarossa (1516–18)		
1520	Jean Florin (1523)	Heyreddin Barbarossa (1516–46)	Wakō piracy (1520–76)	
1540	Robert Reneger (1545)		Xu Dong (1540–48)	Xu Dong (1540s)
	Thomas Wydham (1550s)		Wang Zhi (1545–58)	Wang Zhi (1550s)
	François le Clerc (1553–54)		Hong Dizhen (1555–59)	
			Portuguese raiders (1550s)	
1560	John Hawkins (1562–67)	Euldj Ali (1570–71)	Lin Daoqian (1561–73)	Miguel Lopez de Logazpi (1565)
	Dutch Sea Beggars (1566–1648)			Lin Feng (1570s)
	Francis Drake (1570–95)			Francis Drake (1579)
1580				
1600		John Ward (1603–23)		Oliver van Noot (1600)
		Simon de Danser (1604–09)		Jacob van Heemsberck (1603)
1620	Piet Heyn (1624–28)	Morat Raïs (1620s)	Dutch raiders (1620s–60s)	Zheng Zhilong (1620–46)
	Buccaneers (1630–1680)	Corsairs attack Baltimore (1631)	Zheng Zhilong (1620–46)	
1640		Corsairs in English Channel (1645)	Zheng Chenggong (1640–61)	Zheng Chenggong (1640–61)
			Su Cheng & Su Li (1640–64)	
			Zhou Yu & Li Rong (1663–64)	
1660	François L'Ollonais (1660s)	El-Hadj Hassain (1674–75)		
	Henry Morgan (1663–71)			
1680	Bartholomew Sharpe (1681)	Raïs Venetia (1683)		William Dampier (1680s)
	Henry Every (1694–95)	Sidi Abdallah ben Aïcha (1687–99)		Samuel White (1683)
	William Kidd (1696–99)			Robert Culliford (1696)
1700	Blackbeard (1716–17)	Raïs Hamet Touil (1706)		Woods Rogers (1708)
	Bartholomew Roberts (1718–21)			
	Anne Bonny (1718–21)			
	Mary Read (1718–21)			
1720				
1740		Raïs El-Hadj Embarek (1741–63)		George Anson (1743)
				Raja Ismail (1750s)
1760				
1780		Raïs Hudga Mahomet (1790s)	Taÿson pirates (1780–1802)	Taÿson pirates (1780–1802)
		Raïs Hamidou (1792–1815)	Cai Qian (1790–1809)	Sulu raiders (1780s–1850s)
			Zheng Yi (1790–1807)	Malay raiders (1780s–1850s)
1800			Cai Qian Ma (1800–04)	
			Zheng Yi Sao (1802–10)	
			Zhang Bao (1804–10)	
1820		Raïs Hassan (1824–26)		Chinese pirates (1830s–50s)
1840			Shap-ng-tsai (1840–49)	

Table 1. Comparative Chronology of Piracy, 1500–1850

the ruling elite. In Vietnam in the late eighteenth century, Tâyson rebels encouraged Chinese piracy to help finance their own cause. Piracy was a low-budget method for waging war against one's more powerful and wealthier enemies. Pirates brought revenue to their rulers, officials, and investors, while at the same time they weakened the enemies of the state by attacking their ships and settlements.

While Western governments tried to make sharp legal distinctions between piracy and privateering, in reality distinctions often were blurred. As a latecomer in the race for empire, English governments effectively supported adventurers like Francis Drake and Henry Morgan to plunder Spanish treasure galleons in return for a share of the booty. Though back home the English welcomed Drake and Morgan as heroes, to their Spanish victims they were nothing more than vicious pirates. For the Iranun and Balangingi in insular Southeast Asia in the late eighteenth and early nineteenth centuries, state-sanctioned maritime raiding was a way of life and an honorable profession not only for individuals but also for entire communities. While colonial powers and later historians labeled them as pirates, in fact their activities were much more complex and even critical to the region's emerging political, ethnic, and economic structures. Although the majority of pirates were never authorized by any states, it is important to study those who were for what they can tell us about the role of piracy in state-building and in the global economy.

The main body of the book consists of historical documents and case studies about pirates and piracy. While actual participants wrote many of the included documents, others were written by eyewitnesses and officials. The range of sources here include archival criminal cases, legal depositions and pirate confessions, government reports, memoirs of pirate captives, broadsides, pamphlets, and poems. These primary sources are windows of experience into the world of pirates past. I have selected each document for representativeness, readability, and freshness. This casebook permits readers to metaphorically put on the shoes of historians, allowing them to analyze a set of complex and sometimes contradictory sources in order to solve historical problems. It will also encourage readers to think more critically in distinguishing fact from fancy in pursuing historical research. It is hoped that this book will provide the resources necessary for sharpening analytical skills in defining and solving problems pertinent to today and to the past.

Pirates, Privateers, and Buccaneers of the West

The Age of Discovery, which began in the fifteenth century, was a watershed in world history. Columbus opened the door to the modern world and to an age of Western expansion and domination around the globe. Exploration and expansion also ushered in an age of bitter international rivalries and wars between the Western powers. As the explorers and traders sailed the globe, pirates, privateers, and buccaneers followed in their wake. Often, too, the explorers themselves did not hesitate to engage in maritime marauding. During his fourth voyage to the New World in 1502, Columbus' crew robbed a large native trading vessel off the coast of Honduras. Once the Spanish had firmly established themselves in the Americas, the Caribbean became an international battleground for maritime raiders. For several hundred years European governments actually supported piracy as an inexpensive and effective means of advancing trade and empire, a policy that one historian has called "piratical imperialism."[1]

The sixteenth to eighteenth centuries was a time when international rivalries were intense and wars common among the nations of Europe. Piracy, in one form or another, closely followed the ebb and flow of wars (see Table 2). In wartime, European governments justified piracy under the rubric of privateering and in peacetime they often turned a blind eye to piracy. Privateers were defined legally as vessels belonging to private individuals that received government-issued commissions, often called "letters of marque," authorizing them to attack and plunder enemy shipping during times of war (Doc. 1). The captured vessels and goods, called

---

[1] Peter Earle, *Pirate Wars* (New York: St. Martin's Press, 2003), p. xi.

Years	Pirate Activities	Wars and Key Events
1550s	LeClerc in the West Indies (1553–54)	
1560s	Drake & English Sea Dogs in the Caribbean	Wars of Religion (1562–98)
	Dutch Sea Beggars (1566–1648)	
1570s	Drake attacks Panama (1572)	Battle of Lepanto (1571)
	Drake in the Pacific (1579–80)	
1580s	Dutch Sea Beggars	Anglo-Spanish War (1585–1603)
	Drake in the Caribbean (1586)	(Spanish Armada, 1588)
		Dutch Wars of Independence (1581–1648)
1590s	Drake in the Caribbean (1595–96)	
1600s	Van Noot in the Pacific (1600)	Queen Elizabeth dies (1603)
		James I & peace with Spain (1604)
		Twelve-Years' Truce (1609–21)
1610s		Thirty Years' War (1618–48)
1620s	Piet Heyn in West Indies (1624–28)	
1630s	Buccaneers in Caribbean (1630–80)	
1640s		English Civil War (1642–49)
		Peace of Westphalia (1648)
1650s		English take Jamaica (1655)
1660s	L'Ollonais in the Caribbean	Anglo-Dutch War (1664–68)
	Morgan in the Caribbean	
1670s	Morgan pillages Panama (1671)	Anglo-Dutch War (1672–74)
		King Philip's War (1675–76)
1680s	South Sea Pirates Sharp, Ringrose,	Glorious Revolution in England (1688)
	Davis, and others	Jacobite War (1689–97)
		King William's War (1689–97)
1690s	Red Sea Pirates Every, Kidd, and others	Earthquake destroys Port Royal (1692)
		Peace of Ryswick (1697)
1700s	Kidd executed (1701)	Queen Anne's War (1702–13)
1710s	Blackbeard (1716–18)	Jacobite Rebellions (1715 & 1719)
	Cocklyn in West Africa (1719)	Treaty of Utrecht (1713)
1720s	Roberts, Rackam, Bonny, and Read	Anglo-Spanish War (1727–29)

Table 2. Piracy and War in the West, 1550–1730

"prizes," were then divided between the sanctioning government, investors, captain, and crew. In contrast, piracy was an unauthorized act of violence and predation emanating from the sea against ships or settlements on shore. Pirates owed loyalty to no king, attacked the ships of all nations, and seized booty for personal gain. Although the legal distinctions were clear, actual practice was another matter. The captains and crews who served on privateers and on pirate ships were generally the same—during times of war pirates became privateersmen and in times of peace privateersmen resumed piracy. What one country viewed as legitimate privateering another country—usually the victim—regarded as outright piracy. Moreover, piracy proved to be an important component in state-building. Pirates and privateersmen were viewed as auxiliaries to the navy and a benefit to the national economy because they destroyed the commerce of rival countries. Relatively few pirates were hanged before the eighteenth century. Many, in fact, became national heroes; some were even knighted.

Western piracy was a complicated phenomenon that went through several phases between the late fifteenth and early eighteenth centuries. What began chiefly as localized coastal marauding gradually escalated into a worldwide activity by the end of the seventeenth century. In the first phase, roughly between 1500 and 1600, once news reached Europe of New World Spanish treasures, maritime predators, such as Francis Drake, swarmed the Caribbean. The buccaneers followed between 1630 and 1680. Then in the 1680s to the 1730s, European pirates, having lost their bases in the Caribbean, moved into the Pacific, Indian Ocean, and North Atlantic. Exemplified by such notorious figures as Bartholomew Sharp, Henry Every, William Kidd, and Edward Teach, this last group of pirates became the most numerous and successful of them all. Unlike the other pirates we will discuss in this book, Western pirates were truly global in their activities. There were few areas where they did not venture (Map 1). Not only did the scope of piracy change but so too did the habits and customs of the pirates. Over those three hundred years piracy evolved from state policy to a criminal endeavor inimical to all states. By 1700 pirates were no longer viewed as patriots but as the enemies of mankind as well as of commercial expansion and capitalism.

The Rise of Western Piracy, 1500–1600

In the sixteenth century, because England, Holland, and France were latecomers to empire-building, the best they could hope for was to rob gold and silver from Spanish and Portuguese ships and settlements. Repeated failures to break the Iberian trade monopolies swayed the latecomers to adopt more violent, predatory methods. Two types of piracy developed during the sixteenth century in the West: short-distance piracy operating mainly along the coasts of England and the continent, and oceanic or long-distance piracy, epitomized by Francis Drake and other "gentlemen adventurers." Short-distance piracy had actually existed for centuries before 1500, preying mostly on foreign vessels in the English Channel and off the coasts of Ireland and the continent. Most of the pirates

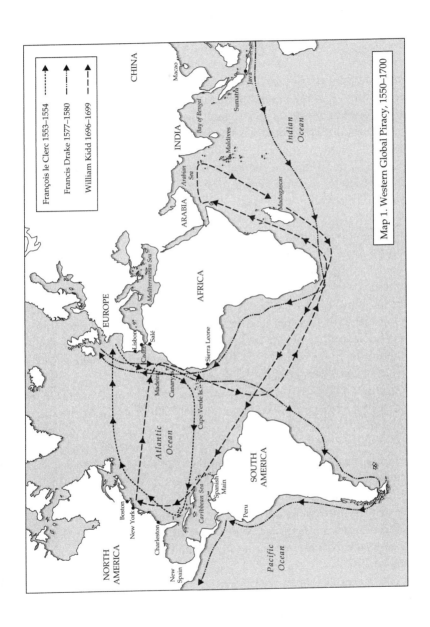

Map 1. Western Global Piracy, 1550–1700

were English and French. As long as the pirates did not attack native shipping, public opinion and state authority paid them little heed. Although piracy was an illegal activity, it was considered useful because it provided communities with cheap goods and employed local toughs who might otherwise have engaged in robbing their neighbors. For many men, however, piracy was a casual occupation entered upon when they could no longer make ends meet from their regular jobs. Many communities became entwined with piracy, as local notables formed syndicates to protect and aid pirates. These magnates usually did not take a direct part in piracy; rather, they put up the money, provided the ships and provisions, and arranged for port facilities by bribing officials. In return for their services the syndicates received the major share—normally four-fifths—of the profits. By the second half of the sixteenth century, however, piracy in northern European waters had greatly diminished, due in part to the growth of power of central governments at the expense of local notables who had been supporting pirates.

By the 1540s coastal piracy began to expand beyond the English Channel following the extension of merchant shipping operations into the Mediterranean and Atlantic. Well-organized pirate fleets followed regular cruising patterns, shadowing the richest trade routes of the day. They set sail from lairs in northern waters in late autumn to plunder the coasts of Spain and Portugal, taking their prizes to Morocco in the winter to sell. Then in the spring they would set sail for Madeira and the Azores, or they would return northward to pillage Newfoundland fisheries. One of the first successful deep-sea pirates was the Frenchman Jean Florin, who robbed Spanish treasure ships off the coast of Portugal in 1523. An English merchant and pirate named Robert Reneger, in 1545, seized Spanish ships and goods in the West Indies. In 1552, the French pirate François le Clerc, known as Jambe de Bois or Peg-leg, raided the Portuguese island of Madeira; a year later he pillaged Spanish Cuba (Map 1).

Whether at war or at peace, maritime raiding against the Spanish in the Caribbean escalated between 1568 and 1603. Motivated by a desire for loot as well as by an intense religious zeal, Protestant English seamen joined forces with Dutch sea-beggars and French

Huguenots in an unofficial sea war against the Spanish "papists." In the 1560s, John Hawkins and Francis Drake entered the Caribbean first as slave traders and later as pirates. They were interlopers who stole African slaves from the Portuguese to sell illegally to Spanish settlers in the Americas. Despite the illegalities and the protests from Spain, their undertakings were backed by Queen Elizabeth. During the two decades before the Anglo-Spanish War (1585–1603), dozens of unsanctioned English Sea Dogs entered the Caribbean with the sole purpose of piracy. The most famous among them was the militant Puritan and fervent nationalist Drake, who led several piratical expeditions in the West Indies between 1570 and 1572, returning home to England in the following year with a small fortune. Several years later, in 1577, when Drake embarked on his famous circumnavigation of the globe, one major objective had been to plunder the Spanish treasure ships and settlements in the Pacific (Doc. 2; Map 1). Regarded as a "heretic and pirate" by the Spaniards, Drake was a hero back home, and in 1581 the queen knighted him. Then during the war years with Spain, Drake and hundreds of privateers set off each year to harass Spanish shipping in the Caribbean. It was not uncommon for them also to seize neutral ships and cargoes, which they quickly and quietly disposed of in Irish or Barbary ports that were beyond the reach of the Admiralty Court in London.[2] Justifiably England became known as a "nation of pirates."

Buccaneers in the Caribbean, 1630–1680

The rise of the buccaneers in the Caribbean coincided with the decline of Spain as a political and economic superpower in Europe. It also coincided with the Cromwell dictatorship in England and the subsequent Restoration of Charles II and the Stuart Dynasty, the rise of Louis XIV in France, and the consolidation of Dutch independence from Spain. The buccaneers were a motley group of French, English, Dutch, and even Spanish and Portuguese renegades and misfits, whose prime targets were Spanish ships and

[2] Before 1662, the Admiralty Court in London had the responsibility to adjudge prizes taken by privateers so they could be lawfully condemned, a process that was necessary before the prizes could be legally shared out.

towns in the Caribbean (Map 2). Buccaneers were the first maritime raiders in the Americas to be universally recognized as pirates. Yet they were distinct from other pirates in that they generally limited their attacks to the Spanish, whereas most pirates attacked everyone. Also unlike the earlier pirates who usually returned to Europe at the end of a raid, the buccaneers preferred to remain in the Caribbean. They consciously separated themselves from their own societies, becoming increasingly independent, and forming their own outlaw communities, calling themselves the Brethren of the Coast (Doc. 3).

Originally buccaneers were not pirates. They were rugged backwoodsmen who lived off the land by hunting feral cattle and pigs for survival; they acquired the name *boucaniers* or *buccaneers* from their method of roasting and preserving meat. They lived on sparsely settled islands on the fringes of the Spanish Empire, in such places as Hispaniola. Later escaped slaves, runaway indentured servants, marooned sailors, and other marginalized elements joined with them. About 1630, a number of buccaneers moved to the tiny island of Tortuga. From this base they began using canoes to harass passing Spanish vessels, gradually expanding their operations with the vessels they had captured. After Tortuga became

Map 2.
The Caribbean Sea in the
Age of Buccaneers

firmly established as a pirate lair, French ships began calling there to trade, and by the 1660s the island had become a French colony.

Besides Tortuga, Jamaica also served as a major base for buccaneers. The English occupied Jamaica in 1655, and soon afterward its chief city, Port Royal, became a rendezvous for desperados from all parts of the West Indies, as well as from Europe. The city gained a reputation as one of the "wickedest towns" in the Americas, a veritable pirate port that rivaled the corsair city of Algiers. Port Royal grew rapidly as a commercial port specializing in stolen goods. Its governors regularly issued privateering commissions, allowing raiding against Spanish vessels, even after the home government had announced peace with Spain in May 1660. In war and peace, local officials and residents supported maritime raiding because it pumped badly needed capital and goods into the island's economy while also offering employment to indigent sailors and drifters. Furthermore, buccaneers provided a costless and effective naval defense against Spanish attacks.

In the sixteen years after the English occupied Jamaica, the buccaneers sacked eighteen Spanish cities, four towns, and over thirty-five villages; they also plundered countless Spanish vessels. Among these pirates was Henry Morgan, who was quickly developing a reputation as a successful buccaneer. During the troubled peace with Spain, in 1668, Morgan received the blessings of Governor Modyford to pillage Puerto Principe in Cuba and later that year Portobello in Panama. Two years later Morgan led over a thousand men to attack Spanish settlements at Santa Marta and Campeche, and then in 1671 he pillaged the great treasure city of Panama itself. Despite his successful campaigns, back in England a number of influential people were beginning to have second thoughts about the benefits of piracy to the realm. Modyford was recalled to London and imprisoned, and two years later Morgan too was called back to England to stand trial for his crimes. Instead of punishment, however, Morgan was rewarded with knighthood, and was soon on his way back to Jamaica as deputy governor. He died a popular hero in Jamaica in 1688.

Even so the winds of change were blowing. After 1677, for the first time, buccaneers were convicted and executed for piracy in the Vice-Admiralty Court in Jamaica. A few years later the Jamaican

FIGURE 1
Morgan Defeats a Spanish Fleet (John Esquemeling, *The Buccaneers of America*. London: George Allen & Company, 1911.)

legislature officially outlawed piracy and the acting governor, Henry Morgan, actually sent out ships to pursue pirates. Jamaican piracy declined only after the island's landowners decided that growing sugar was more profitable than handling pirate booty. Then in 1692, Port Royal was devastated by an earthquake. By then Caribbean buccaneering was practically dead. The centuries of repeated raids on Spanish shipping and towns had so thoroughly ravaged the region that there was little left to pillage.

The Golden Age of Western Piracy, 1680–1730

Beginning in the 1680s those governments that had once supported, or at least tolerated, pirates now found no use for them and began to suppress their activities in the Caribbean and around the globe. The former "patriotic heroes" had become the "villains of all nations." In contrast to the Sea Dogs and buccaneers of earlier times, pirates now began attacking ships and towns regardless of nationality. Between the 1680s and 1730s, Western piracy became global in scope and pirate crews more cosmopolitan in their composition. As suppression in the Caribbean intensified, pirates scattered elsewhere, seeking friendly ports in the Bahamas and in the North American colonies. Some pirates began raiding expeditions in the Pacific. Others, in the 1690s, ventured into the Indian Ocean. In the early decades of the eighteenth century another generation of pirates returned to the North Atlantic to plunder the lucrative colonial trade. Each new wave of piracy, however, was met with increasingly harsher and more determined extermination campaigns, so that by 1730 Western piracy had been virtually eliminated around the world.

One glaring problem in the suppression of pirates, however, was the support that they received from various colonial officials and merchants. The Bahamas remained a favorite pirate haunt until the English government finally sent Woods Rogers, himself once a privateersman, in 1718 to clear the islands of pirates. Armed with ships of the Royal Navy and the king's pardon, Rogers' two-pronged strategy eliminated the pirates within two years. The North American colonies, which were quite reluctant to give up the lucrative pirate trade, were more difficult to deal with. Pirates of all nations had little problem fitting out ships, selling loot, and recruiting crews in the friendly ports of New York, Rhode Island, Massachusetts, and the Carolinas (Docs. 4 and 5). American colonists viewed the pirates, according to Patrick Pringle, as "free-traders running the blockade of the Navigation Acts."[3] Because the Navigation Acts, which required all colonial imports and exports to be carried on English vessels, greatly limited trade and profits, colonialists sought to evade the laws by doing business with smugglers and pirates.

Although ever since the time of Drake pirates had been combing the Pacific for the fabled Manila galleons, starting in the 1680s, with fewer opportunities in the West Indies for plunder, pirates stepped up their operations in the Pacific. One of those pirates was an experienced buccaneer named Bartholomew Sharp. He and his men sank twenty-five Spanish ships, killed over two hundred people, and made off with over 200,000 pesos worth of loot, including

[3] Patrick Pringle, *Jolly Roger: The Story of the Great Age of Piracy* (New York: W. W. Norton, 1953), p. 137.

valuable maps he had stolen from the Spaniards. Afterward Sharp's gang dispersed; some went to the Bahamas while others went to the Carolinas, where they joined up with Edward Davis aboard the *Revenge*. They set out in August 1683 with a crew of seventy pirates, intending to plunder the Pacific. En route, off the coast of Sierra Leone, they first captured a slave ship, which had on board sixty African females; the pirates quickly exchanged ships and renamed their prize the *Bachelor's Delight*. For the next five years Davis cruised the Pacific coast of Spanish America, but never took anything of substantial value. Later, in 1689, after Davis had departed, the *Bachelor's Delight* (now commanded by Capt. Raynor) quit the Pacific for the Indian Ocean, and after a successful voyage—worth some £80,000 in booty—she sailed back for the Carolinas in 1692 (Doc. 4). The Pacific proved to be such a vast theater of operations for pirating that in the two centuries between 1550 and 1750, only four Manila galleons were ever captured.

If pirates had difficulties finding rich prizes in the Pacific, this was not the case in the Indian Ocean. The occasion for the rise of Western piracy in southwestern Asia was the decline of the Mogul Empire (1526–1761) in India and the concomitant increase in European trade in the region. Although at first the pirates chiefly attacked Muslim ships—"no sin for Christians to rob heathens"[4]— soon they also were robbing European merchant vessels. Each year Muslim fleets of twenty or more ships traveled from Surat to Mocha at the mouth of the Red Sea, carrying thousands of pilgrims on route to Mecca. On their return to India the ships were laden with rich cargoes of gold, silver, silks, and jewels. The large, poorly armed, and slow-moving Mogul ships fell easy prey to the well-armed and ravenous pirates. Once they filled their ships with plunder the pirates sought out friendly ports where they could easily dispose of their loot to eager buyers.

Henry Every (or Avery) and William Kidd were two of the most famous Red Sea pirates. The two men were transitional figures whose outlaw careers occurred right at the time when attitudes

[4] The quote comes from Philip Gosse's *The History of Piracy* (Glorieta, N.M.: Rio Grande Press, 1995), p. 177, paraphrasing the words of Darby Mullins, who sailed with Captain Kidd to the Indian Ocean in 1697.

toward pirates were changing not only in Europe but also in the colonies. Every, who probably began his outlaw career as a South Sea buccaneer, plundered two rich Muslim pilgrim ships in 1695 near the Red Sea, which allotted to each crewman a fortune of £1,000. While several of his men were eventually apprehended, tried, and hanged, Every slipped away and vanished from the pages of history (Doc. 5). Kidd was not so fortunate. At the time that Every was pillaging the Orient, Kidd was in London obtaining commissions from the king to hunt down enemy French vessels and Red Sea pirates (Doc. 6). Outfitted in England with a new vessel, the *Adventure Galley*, Kidd set sail for the Indian Ocean in 1696, reaching Madagascar in January 1697. Soon afterward, Kidd apparently crossed the thin line separating privateer and pirate. In the Indian Ocean he attacked several European vessels and in January 1698 he robbed the Mogul ship, the *Quedah Merchant*. By the time he returned to New York in the following spring, much of the booty had already been distributed and he found himself a wanted man (Map 1). Kidd had set off on his long voyage as a privateersman but returned home a pirate. He was arrested and sent to England, and in a showcase trial found guilty of piracy and murder and hanged in May 1701.

Following Kidd's execution there was a temporary lull in piracy that coincided with Queen Anne's War (1702–1713). Privateering, as expected, rose during hostilities. Once the war ended, however, piracy surged as thousands of sailors were thrown out of work. During this last great pirate cycle, that lasted through the 1720s, there were over 5,000 pirates, many made famous in Captain Charles Johnson's *A General History of the Pyrates*, first published in 1724. This was the age of Edward Teach, the infamous Blackbeard, who terrorized the American coast in 1716–1717, and went into battle with a sling of pistols over his shoulder and "lighted matches under his hat." Perhaps less famous, but equally colorful and a lot more successful, was Bartholomew Roberts—Black Bart—who wore gaudy silk garments and captured over four hundred ships before his death in 1722. There was also the pirate Thomas Cocklyn, who received a royal pardon in 1717 in the Bahamas, but soon afterwards was back at his old trade. Off the

FIGURE 2
Blackbeard the Pirate (Charles Johnson, *A General History of the Lives and Adventures of the Most Famous Highwaymen, Murderers, Street Robbers, &c.* London: Printed for and sold by O. Payne, 1736. New York Public Library, Rare Books Division.)

coast of West Africa, in 1719, he captured a slave ship commanded by William Snelgrave, who described the pirate as a villainous captain chosen "on account of his Brutality and Ignorance" (Doc. 7).

Among the thousands of male pirates of the early eighteenth century, we have information on only two female pirates, Anne Bonny and Mary Read, and what little information we have on them comes chiefly from Johnson's *History of the Pyrates* mentioned above. There were certainly other women pirates, but because they dressed and acted as men aboard ship we know very little about them. We know about Bonny and Read because in 1720 they were apprehended, put on trial in Jamaica, and, having been found guilty of piracy, sentenced to death (though both were reprieved because they were "quick with child"). These two feisty women, who served with John Rackam (alias Calico Jack) in the Atlantic and West Indies for several years, cussed and fought with the toughest of the men pirates (Doc. 8; also Stanley's essay in Part 3). Given the scarcity of women at sea, historian B. R. Burg has argued that homosexuality was common aboard pirate ships.[5] The evidence, however, neither proves nor disproves his argument. Undoubtedly some sailors and pirates engaged in sodomy, or what was then called "buggery," because of sexual orientation, while others—particularly young cabin boys—did so because of coercion from ship's officers. Nevertheless, homosexual activities aboard ship did not preclude heterosexual activities on shore, as seamen worldwide had reputations for their lusty habits.

Over the course of the centuries the social composition and nature of piracy changed dramatically. During the first phase, pirates were led mostly by petty nobles and "gentlemen adventurers" and gangs were organized along rigid hierarchical lines. They were neither democratic in the manning of ships nor the distribution of booty. Gangs too were divided chiefly along national lines. Later, in the seventeenth and early eighteenth centuries, nearly all pirates had been born into the lowest social classes and many were in fact "desperate Rogues." The great majority were single men in their mid-twenties. Most crews were a veritable mix of Europeans, Africans, and native Americans. The pirates of this later age were decidedly opposed to established political and religious authorities and conventional society. As Marcus Rediker has argued, pirates created a democratic and egalitarian social order that stood in "defiant contradistinction to the ways of the world they left behind."[6] They bonded themselves together in social compacts, normally as written articles agreed upon by all crewmen at the outset of a voyage. These articles, which defined gangs as cohesive,

[5] B. R. Burg, *Sodomy and the Pirate Tradition: English Sea Rovers in the Seventeenth-Century Caribbean* (New York: New York University Press, 1984).

[6] Marcus Rediker, *Between the Devil and the Deep Blue Sea: Merchant Seamen, Pirates, and the Anglo-American Maritime World, 1700–1750* (New York: Cambridge University Press, 1987), p. 267.

self-governing bodies, detailed the allocation of authority, enforcement of discipline, and distribution of loot (Doc. 9). Aboard pirate ships the majority ruled. Captains were elected and were answerable to their crews, who also voted on all important matters. Booty was pooled into a "common chest" and equitably distributed among officers and men (Docs. 7 and 9; also Rediker's essay in Part 3). Pirates created an alternative society that "presented a threat not only to property but to the developing national state and its way of organizing politics and society."[7]

Pirate antisocial behavior was matched by a brutal war on piracy. Pirates found themselves increasingly isolated in a hostile world. Their former colonial supporters abandoned the pirates when they started robbing ships carrying exports from the colonies. While few pirates had been executed before 1700, scores would be hanged each year thereafter. Piratical imperialism was replaced by mercantile imperialism, whereby states condemned piracy and promoted trade. There was no longer a place for free-thinking, individualistic maritime marauders on the periphery of empire. The state would demand its monopoly of violence at sea. A combination of relentless suppression campaigns, swift trials, mass executions, and royal pardons soon brought an end to the great age of piracy in the West, but not elsewhere in the world.

Corsairs, Renegades, and Slaves in the Mediterranean

With the rise of the Atlantic world the ancient Mediterranean world slipped slowly into decline. By the early sixteenth century the Mediterranean Sea was no longer the chief waterway for international commerce or for the distribution of Oriental goods to Europe. The Portuguese had opened a southern route to Asia via the Indian Ocean and the Spanish had discovered a New World in

[7] Janice E. Thomson, *Mercenaries, Pirates, and Sovereigns: State-Building and Extraterritorial Violence in Early Modern Europe* (Princeton: Princeton University Press, 1994), p. 46.

the Americas. Nevertheless, for the next century or so old Mediterranean trade routes continued to compete fairly well with the new oceanic routes. Ships from all over Europe continued to call at Mediterranean ports. For Ottoman and other Muslim merchants the Mediterranean Sea remained vital to trade and prosperity. Earlier in the fifteenth century, as the two great superpowers of the age, the Ottoman and Spanish Empires, expanded further into the Mediterranean, rivalry exploded into war. In 1492, as Columbus made his way to America, the Spanish rulers expelled the Moors[8] from their soil and soon afterward began seizing footholds in North Africa, including Algiers, Tunis, and Tripoli. Although Ottoman expansion in western Europe came to an end with the failure to seize Vienna in 1529, and with the defeat of the Turkish fleet at Lepanto in 1571, the Ottoman sultans had managed to recover their losses in North Africa by 1574.

The Battle of Lepanto, however, proved to be a watershed in Mediterranean history. Afterward both Turkish and Spanish rulers turned their attention elsewhere and disengaged themselves from overt warfare in the Mediterranean. Spain under Philip II became increasingly concerned with rivalries inside Europe while Turkish rulers became concerned with Persia and internal dissentions within their own empire. The great naval wars between the two adversaries devolved into proxy wars of piracy, which reached a peak in the seventeenth century. With the weakening of the sultanate, the Barbary city-states of Algiers, Tunis, and Tripoli became virtually independent corsair regimes. Christian religious orders, such as the Knights of St. John of Jerusalem, carried on maritime crusades from strongholds on the island of Malta and elsewhere. In the meantime, Protestant England and Holland, through a combination of trade and piracy, began to challenge the predominance of Catholic Spain in the Mediterranean and around the globe. From the seventeenth century onward for the next two hundred years, various complex forms of maritime predation were facts of everyday life in the Mediterranean (Map 3). The conflict in the Mediterranean had become as much about religion as it was about trade and politics.

---

[8] Moors were Muslim conquerors that had occupied Spain since the eighth century.

Between the sixteenth and nineteenth centuries, corsairing went
through three distinct stages: first a period of growth and development during the sixteenth century, followed by a golden age in the

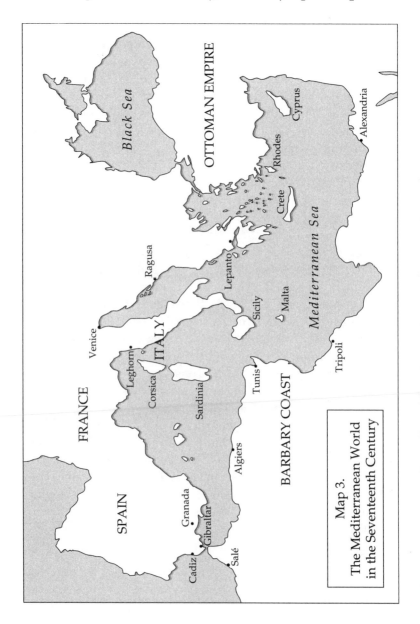

Map 3.
The Mediterranean World
in the Seventeenth Century

next century, and then a long period of stagnation and decline over the eighteenth and early nineteenth centuries.

The Rise of the Mediterranean Corsairs, 1500–1600

Maritime marauding was nothing new to the Mediterranean in the sixteenth century. It predated ancient Greece and Rome. After a decline in the Middle Ages, piracy once again was on the rise with the revival of seaborne trade in the thirteenth century. The threat to trade, however, was only sporadic as the outlaws lacked the protection of any state; at this stage they were mostly petty gangs of pirates, owing loyalty to no king and attacking virtually everyone. Gradually over the course of the fifteenth century, as the Holy War between Muslims and Christians spilled over into the Mediterranean Sea, groups of corsairs expanded their activities with the support of rulers on both sides of the conflict. The expulsion of the Moors from Spain in 1492 proved to be a tremendous boost to the corsair ranks. Unemployed, destitute, and vengeful, many of them readily took work as corsairs and revenged themselves by attacking Spanish ships and settlements. Then in the early sixteenth century, with Spanish penetration into North Africa, Algiers turned to the Ottoman corsair, Aruj, who entered the city in 1516. He and his younger brother, Heyreddin, eventually drove the Spaniards from Algiers and became the masters of the city. The two Barbarossa brothers, as they were known in the West, laid the foundations for the rise of the Barbary corsairs as a menacing force in the Mediterranean.

The brothers were members of a corsairing family that hailed from the island of Mitylene off the Turkish coast. Their father was probably a renegade and a corsair.[9] He had four sons who followed in his footsteps. Aruj, the eldest son, after first serving in the Turkish navy, later turned to the corsairing profession, where he quickly made a name for himself. In 1492 he helped transport the fleeing Moors to North Africa. Nine years later, while fighting Christian corsairs, Aruj was taken prisoner and forced to serve as a galley

---

[9] Renegades were persons who deserted their faith for another. The term *corsair* is ambiguous. Derived from the word *corsaro*, in Mediterranean languages it denoted a privateer, but in English it denoted a pirate.

FIGURE 3

The Dangers of Mediterranean Seafaring (William Okeley, *Eben-Ezer, or a Small Monument of Great Mercy*, London: Printed for Nat. Ponder, 1675. Folger Shakespeare Library.)

slave for three years before being ransomed. Although he captured many Spanish vessels, his most famous exploit was the taking of two large galleys belonging to Pope Julius II. As Aruj's reputation grew, Turkish and renegade adventurers flocked to his banner. By 1510 he commanded a squadron of ten to twelve vessels. He died fighting the Spanish in Algiers in 1518.

After Aruj's death, the youngest brother, Heyreddin, continued to expand corsair power in the region. He shrewdly allied himself with the Ottoman sultan, who appointed him as the beylerbey or viceroy of Algiers and some years later as "grand admiral" in the Turkish navy. By the 1530s he was the unchallenged master of Algiers, having driven the Spanish from much of the Barbary coast. By then he had a corsair navy of over 2,000 men and some sixty galleys. Each spring, as the weather settled, his fleet set off from Algiers to plunder Christian shipping in the Mediterranean. In 1534 his galleys methodically prowled along the coasts of Sicily and Italy, pillaging towns and carrying away their inhabitants to put into slavery, and in the next year his fleets attacked and captured Tunis. A superb seaman and fearless fighter, he had a reputation for invincibility. He was the terror of the Mediterranean, attacking not only lone vessels but also entire fleets. In 1538 and again in 1541, his forces defeated Spanish armadas under the famous Admiral Andrea Doria. By the time of Heyreddin's death in 1546, piracy had become a well-established instrument of state policy in Algiers.

Under Heyreddin, Algiers had become the most formidable corsair stronghold and the leading port in North Africa. The city, which had a population of between 100,000 and 150,000, was a mixture of Africans, Turks, Jews, Moors, Greeks, and renegades from Christendom. Despite the city's growth, its economy suffered from basic structural defects, due in large measure to its dependence on corsair activities. Although a vibrant commercial hub, most of the trade at Algiers was carried on by European merchants and the corsairs themselves. In fact, corsairs were not only the basis for trade but also the most important source of revenue. Moreover, because Algiers, like the rest of the Barbary coast, was underpopulated, it relied on Christian renegades and captives to prop up the economy. Prisoners, whether held for labor or for ransom, were the most important booty.

By the late sixteenth century, Barbary corsairs were operating out of Algiers, Tunis, and Tripoli as state-run enterprises. Each city had established well-organized systems for the recruiting, organizing, and financing of corsairs. Much of the public finances, in fact, depended on the state's share of corsair prizes. The corsairs were organized into mercantile companies called *taïfa al-raïs*, whose motives were mostly economic. Organized like joint-stock companies, investors in the *taïfa al-raïs* came from all walks of life—merchants, government officials, janissary officers, ship captains, shopkeepers, craftsmen, seamen, and ordinary citizens. Booty was carefully noted on detailed inventories before being sold as legitimately acquired gains in Muslim as well as in Christian ports, such as Leghorn and Amsterdam. Jewish merchants, who were scattered throughout the Mediterranean and Europe, were the chief brokers in the sale of stolen goods and slaves. The dependence on corsairs made the *raïs* (captains) a powerful factor in both government and society.

At the same time that Barbary states were forming close ties with corsairs, on the northern shores of the Mediterranean Christian potentates were also busy organizing their own corsair forces to plunder Muslim shipping. Not only the King of Spain, but also his dependencies, the Viceroy of Sicily and the Grand Duke of Tuscany, issued corsairing commissions. The Christian forces were led by the crusading order of the Knights of St. John of Jerusalem, which after being driven off the island of Rhodes by the Turks, settled on Malta in 1530. Its Grand Master also issued licenses to corsairs (Doc. 10). At that time the island was an impoverished Spanish fiefdom. The Knights of Malta, as they were better known, carried on their Holy War long after the Crusades had ended. They fortified the island and built a new navy. Although their chief targets were Muslim ships plying the eastern Mediterranean, nevertheless, when opportunity arose, Maltese corsairs also plundered Christian vessels. Besides plundering the cargo, they also kidnapped crews and passengers for ransom and for sale into slavery. Oftentimes Christian Greek settlements in the Mediterranean were pillaged not only by Muslim but also by Christian corsairs (Doc. 11).

Although bitter enemies, there were many similarities between the corsairs of Barbary and Malta. They were in both instances state-sponsored enterprises. The rulers themselves outfitted corsair ships or alternatively they issued licenses to private individuals to outfit vessels, which in return provided a share of the booty to the state: normally one-eighth in Barbary and one-tenth in Malta. Corsairing was regarded as a legal and honorable profession and one that was vital to the economies on both sides of the Mediterranean. Slaves and ships were the two most valued prizes in Barbary and in Malta. Moreover, corsairs were deeply entrenched in politics and society, with corsair captains being vital members of the ruling class. Both Muslim and Christian corsairs also shared their prizes with their respective religious clerics: Barbary corsairs with the marabouts who prayed for their success in battle and Maltese corsairs with the nuns of the Convent of St. Ursula who prayed ceaselessly for victory over the infidel.

The Golden Age of the Barbary Corsairs, 1600–1650

Beginning in the seventeenth century the nature of Mediterranean corsairing changed. Both the number of Barbary corsairs and the scope of their activities had greatly expanded. This was due in large measure to the injection of new blood into their ranks from north European renegades and from Moriscos[10] from Spain. During the first half of the seventeenth century there were perhaps as many as 20,000 corsairs operating from North African ports. Their fleets likewise became stronger and better organized. By this time, too, corsairing had ceased being an exclusively Mediterranean activity as it spread into the Atlantic. The seventeenth century—especially the first half—was the golden age of the corsairs.

The Battle of Lepanto in 1571, followed by the defeat of the Spanish Armada in 1588, marked major changes in the balance of power in the Mediterranean and in Europe as a whole. In their aftermaths the West witnessed the rise of northern Europe, particularly England and Holland as sea powers, and the decline of the Ottoman and Spanish Empires. The first Dutch and English adventurers in the Mediterranean were traders who never hesitated to use force to increase profits. For them piracy was of secondary importance. Later, by the start of the seventeenth century, they

[10] Moriscos were the Muslim (Moor) converts to Christianity who lived in Spain before being expelled in 1609.

were operating in heavily armed vessels specifically for commerce raiding. Their chief motive now was plunder. The changes became apparent after 1603, once James came to the throne in England and ended hostilities with Spain. He quickly reversed his predecessor's policies by expelling English and Dutch pirates and privateers from his coasts. Not too long afterward, thousands of Dutch sailors and soldiers were thrown out of work as the results of the Twelve Years Truce with Spain (1609–1621) and the development of the flute or flyboat, which, because it made the shipping of cargo more economical and efficient, caused scores of seamen to lose their jobs. Many of these men drifted into the Mediterranean and joined the Barbary corsairs.

Once in the Mediterranean these adventurers entered into close working relationships with Muslim corsairs. Many of these Europeans apostatized, that is converted to Islam or, in the language of the day, "turned Turk." At the start of the seventeenth century there were anywhere from 9,000 to 15,000 renegades—mostly men but also some women—living in Barbary cities. While many of them had been abducted before converting, others had voluntarily embraced Islam in the expectation of a better life. Many of the renegades were poor seafarers like John Ward (Doc. 12), who easily became corsairs. Although many captains were English or Dutch, crews were normally a mix of Turkish, North African, and European sailors.

European renegades contributed to the Barbary corsairs not only in needed manpower but also in new military and naval technology. The most important single contribution was the introduction of the so-called "round ships" or sailing ships as a complement to the traditionally oar-powered galleys. This innovation allowed corsairs to expand their range of activities into the Atlantic, where they were soon conducting raids as far away as the English Channel, Iceland, and Newfoundland. The number of attacks increased dramatically: between 1613 and 1621 corsairs took 447 Dutch, 193 French, 120 Spanish, 60 English, and 56 German ships, which were all taken to Algiers as prizes. It was during these years, too, that the Barbary corsairs reached the peak of their power.

Sailing vessels, however, never completely replaced slave-powered galleys in the Mediterranean. In fact, galleys remained the major

FIGURE 4
Selling Christians at the Slave Market in Algiers (Peter Earl, *Corsairs of Malta and Barbary*, 1970. Illustration from British Museum.)

component not only of the Barbary navy but also of the French, Spanish, Italian, and Turkish navies until the early eighteenth century. Therefore, there was a constant demand for slaves to work the oars. Most slaves, who were considered prisoners of war, were captives taken from ships or coastal towns. Not all slaves worked on galleys; many of them also were needed in construction, agriculture, and domestic service. The slave trade was highly organized, so much so that prospective buyers placed advanced orders with corsairs, specifying the number, gender, and skills they most desired. Prisoners were sold in slave markets which were located in all the major ports around the Mediterranean. Like other merchandise, prisoners were displayed in public for three days before being offered for sale. When slaves were bought buyers and sellers drew up sales contracts. In Barbary, slaves were held in prisons called *bagnios*, where they returned each night after a full day's work (Doc. 13). Slaves were not only a vital source of manpower but also vital to the economy for the substantial sums paid for their ransom. Redemption, indeed, was a big business, so much so that it can be argued that the rescue of captives actually helped to perpetuate corsairing and slavery in the Mediterranean into the early nineteenth century.

The Decline of Corsairing, 1680–1830

By the late seventeenth century corsairing began to stagnate and then slowly decline before collapsing in 1830. The very success of the corsairs, in fact, led to their undoing. As the menace to trade and travel multiplied each year, the emerging powers of northern Europe could no longer afford to ignore the problem. Beginning in the 1680s, as we already have noted, the free and easy attitudes that European governments had toward maritime raiding began to harden. But rather than joining forces to eradicate the corsairs, European powers individually negotiated treaties with each of the Barbary regimes. As long as the corsairs attacked the shipping of rival states, they helped eliminate competition. In fact, the English, Dutch, and French actually encouraged Barbary corsairs to continue their warfare on their enemies. They did so in their own interest and in the context of the political and commercial rivalries among themselves. For peace and protection against attack, European governments paid the corsairs tribute, chiefly in the form of money as well as in ships, naval supplies, and weapons. For the Barbary states, which relied on revenues derived from corsairing, tribute became a necessary substitute. Rulers promised to restrain corsair attacks on the ships and ports of the tribute-paying countries. The ships of those countries that did not pay for protection—usually smaller and weaker states—continued to be attacked. The overall effect, however, was a plunge in corsairing activities.

One of those small, weak countries was the fledgling United States, which had gained its independence from England after 1776. As English colonies, American shipping received the same protections as the mother country. The cost of independence, however, meant a loss of treaty protection and American shipping quickly came under attack. Like other countries the United States had to pay tribute for protection or seek other solutions. Between 1794 and 1815 the Americans used a carrot-and-stick approach to solving the Barbary problem: alternating naval expeditions to punish those Barbary states whose corsairs harassed shipping followed by the payments of large indemnities to those states in exchange for peace. In 1794 the United States negotiated a treaty with Algiers, promising to pay $642,500 for the ransom of nearly a hundred prisoners and an annual tribute of $21,600 in naval stores. One of those American captives, John Foss, later wrote about his experiences in captivity as a Barbary slave (Doc. 13). Seven years later America sent warships into the Mediterranean to try to force a peace on her own terms, but the attempt ended in failure when one of the warships was captured and its crew held for ransom. These and later actions marked the wars with Tripoli (1801–1805) and Algiers (1815), which have been recently dubbed America's first wars against terrorism.

In the meantime, during the Napoleonic Wars (1795–1815), the corsairing days of the Knights of Malta came to an end, and once the wars ended the European powers put aside their differences to address the remaining problems of the Barbary corsairs. Several countries dispatched navies into the Mediterranean to protect shipping and to attack pirate strongholds. In 1816 an Anglo-Dutch fleet bombarded Algiers. Nonetheless, it was not until 1830, after a French army occupied Algiers, that the activity of Barbary corsairs came to an end.

What are we to make of these Mediterranean corsairs? Were they pirates or privateers? These are not easy questions to answer. On the one hand, like privateers, the corsairs of Barbary and Malta were duly authorized by states to attack maritime commerce. On the other hand, while privateers were licensed only in time of war to capture or destroy enemy vessels, in the Mediterranean wars were rarely officially declared between Muslims and Christians. Instead, there was a long continuous Holy War. In any case, the enemy was ill-defined and unclear. Barbary corsairs attacked not only Christian ships but occasionally the ships of rival Muslim states. Likewise the Maltese corsairs sometimes plundered Christian ships. Furthermore, the Barbary states which issued corsairing licenses were not independent sovereign nations, but rather dependencies of the Ottoman Empire. Although by the late sixteenth century they were relatively independent, they nevertheless were ostensibly ruled by the sultan in Constantinople. The situation was much the same with Malta, which was a dependency of Hapsburg Spain. The problem involves who had sovereignty and thereby the authority to issue privateering licenses.

To the people involved in corsairing, however, these distinctions were somewhat meaningless and a better approach would be to place the corsairs within the larger context of the early modern political economy. Over much of the same period, European states were also employing privateers—in both war and peace—to engage in the same sorts of activities as the Mediterranean corsairs. Piracy and privateering had become integral components not only of state policy but also of the economy. According to Peter Earle, Barbary and Maltese corsairs were underpinned by "a very sophisticated commercial network of merchants, sea captains, and ransom brokers whose activities spread through the Mediterranean world"[11] and western Europe. Both Christian and Muslim merchants were attracted to Barbary ports in search of stolen goods and slaves at bargain prices. Barbary corsairs openly traded their booty at major Western marts, such as Leghorn and Amsterdam. Many European merchants also financed privateering ventures in the Mediterranean, disregarding all religious and national boundaries. Frequently too, the same people who backed privateering activities simultaneously insured vessels from corsair attacks. In this way corsairing and commerce had become indistinguishable, and religion perhaps merely an excuse for piracy.

Pirates, Merchants, and Rebels on the China Coast

At a time when piracy was waxing and waning in other areas around the globe, in China the golden age of piracy extended for over three hundred years from the sixteenth to the nineteenth centuries. During those years there was an unprecedented growth in Chinese piracy, unsurpassed in size and scope anywhere else in the world. As elsewhere, piracy in China arose during a time of tremendous commercial growth. Piracy surged in three great waves: first there were the merchant-pirates from 1520 to 1574; they were followed by bands of rebels and pirates between 1620 and 1684; and lastly there were the large associations of commoner seafaring pirates from 1780 to 1810. The three great pirate cycles

---

[11] Earle, p. 51.

were characterized by the rise of huge leagues whose power surpassed that of the imperial state in China's maritime world (Map 4). While in the West at its peak in 1720 the pirate population had

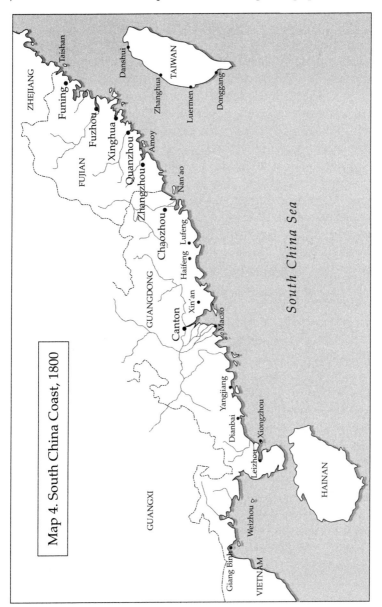

Map 4. South China Coast, 1800

never exceeded 5,500 men, in China the number of pirates was no less than 70,000 at its height in 1809. Never before in history had piracy been so powerful and menacing.

The Wakō Pirates, 1520–1574

The great age of Chinese piracy commenced in the middle of the Ming dynasty (1368–1644) during the reign of the Jiajing Emperor (r. 1522–1566). Beginning in the early 1520s, China witnessed a steady growth in the number of piracies along the coast, and within two decades numerous small gangs had expanded into larger, better-organized fleets. Cresting in the 1550s, at a time when the Ming navy was in decline and the dynasty was facing a serious threat on the northern frontier from resurgent Mongol armies under Altan Khan, pirates challenged imperial authority along the coast. This was also a time of civil war in Japan, when sailors and masterless samurai took to the sea as raiders. Characterized by Ming officials as "dwarf outlaws" (*wokou* or *wakō*), a term used pejoratively for Japanese pirates, they in fact included virtually all pirates operating in China's waters.[12] *Wakō* bands were composed of motley crews of Japanese, Chinese, Southeast Asian, European, and even African rovers and renegades. Using swift sailing vessels they plundered shipping and pillaged port towns from China to Malaya.

A major underlying reason for the sudden upsurge in piracy in the 1520s was the Jiajing Emperor's determination to enforce rigidly the existing sea bans and to enact tough new ones. The imperial court outlawed all private overseas trade and instead hopelessly attempted to restrict maritime commerce within the narrow confines of the tributary system. Anyone caught building large oceangoing junks, trading with foreigners, traveling abroad without authorization, or colluding with smugglers was to be treated as a pirate and when caught executed. Instead of curbing illegal activities, however, the bans actually furthered them. Because tribute missions were infrequent and the amounts of imports and exports

---

[12] *Wokou* is the Chinese pronunciation and *wakō* is the Japanese pronunciation. As early as 1223, Japanese pirates who raided the Korean coast were being labeled *wokou*. They reached their zenith along the China coast during the Jiajing reign.

FIGURE 5
Ming Dynasty Pirate Craft (*Gujin tushu jicheng*, 1884.)

severely limited, they satisfied neither Chinese nor foreign merchants. As a result illicit trade quickly expanded up and down the coast to meet the growing demands. Piracy became the most vivid expression of opposition to official maritime policies and the most important means of conducting seaborne trade.

The Jiajing Emperor's enforcement of the sea bans criminalized large segments of the maritime population. Gradually all strata of coastal society, from fishermen and sailors to merchants and gentry, became involved in illegal enterprises. In the words of one official, "pirates and merchants are all the same people: when markets are open the pirates become merchants and when markets are closed merchants become pirates."[13] Merchant pirates, such as Xu Hai, Wang Zhi, and Hong Dizhen, mixed trade with smuggling and pillaging, organized large fleets, and established bases on offshore islands (Doc. 14). A number of pirate gangs sought protection from influential families and local officials, and many merchants and gentry financed the activities of pirate bands. At the height of the disturbances between 1550 and 1574, most of the South China seaboard had slipped away from Ming control and into the hands of powerful pirates and their gentry supporters.

When the Portuguese first sailed into the South China Sea they came as traders and adventurers, and many acted as pirates. From bases in Southeast Asia they traded clandestinely with Chinese and Japanese pirates and smugglers. In this age of empire building and commercial rivalry, trade and piracy were often indistinguishable, and several Western governments, as we have already noted, maintained tolerant attitudes toward piracy, viewing it as an important auxiliary to legitimate trade. Limitless opportunities in Asia for riches, either through trade or pillage, attracted European renegades and adventurers to the region. At the time that the Portuguese were establishing a foothold in Macao (1554), their traders not only engaged in commerce but also pillaged Chinese villages and carried off women and children who were sold into slavery. In fact, at about this time a number of Portuguese fortune hunters were arrested, tried, and executed as pirates in Fujian province.

Erratic *wakō* raids continued along the South China coast into the early seventeenth century, but after 1574 the number of incidents dramatically decreased. After the Jiajing Emperor died in 1567, his successor removed the sea bans on all but the Japanese, and Chinese overseas trade was legalized although still restricted. Several major pirate leaders were killed in battle, surrendered to the state, or fled to Southeast Asia. In addition, the political reunification of Japan in the latter part of the sixteenth century did much to curtail Japanese piracy in the whole region. As China's economy finally stabilized between 1570 and 1620, more and more

---

[13] Cited in Jiang Zhuyuan and Fang Zhiqin, eds., *Jianming Guangdong shi* [*A brief history of Guangdong*] (Guangzhou: Guangdong People's Press, 1993), p. 263.

people discarded piracy for legitimate trade. With markets open pirates again became merchants.

Pirates and Rebels, 1620–1684

After a hiatus of about fifty years, a new wave of large-scale piracy surged forth during the Ming-Qing dynastic wars between 1620 and 1684, with piracy reaching a peak in the 1640s to 1660s. Often characterized in official accounts as "sea rebels" (*haini*), the pirate upsurge was symptomatic of the general crisis in China which accompanied the change of dynasties. Given the economic and political anarchy of this period, a clear distinction between piracy, rebellion, and trade was impossible. The Zheng family, taking advantage of the instability, built a maritime empire in South China based on a combination of trade, piracy, and political intrigue. Other pirates joined with bandits and rebels to attack markets and walled cities. European traders, with the continued support of their governments, also took advantage of the turmoil in China to pillage ports and merchant junks.

By the 1620s the relative stability and prosperity of the previous several decades had been abruptly shattered. Externally, Manchu incursions on the northeastern frontier challenged Ming sovereignty and forced the government to commit large amounts of money and troops to defend the border, thereby weakening its military presence along the coast. Internally, corruption, factionalism, incompetence, and fiscal bankruptcy crippled the Ming state. Although the imperial court had opened foreign trade in 1567, after 1623 it once again began to intermittently prohibit maritime trade, finally banning it altogether in 1626 (except for a brief period between 1631–1632). At the same time the Chinese economy stagnated and then declined, as foreign trade came to a standstill and prices skyrocketed. Pirates once again appeared everywhere along the coast.

Beginning in the 1620s the Zheng family, first under Zheng Zhilong and then under his son Zheng Chenggong (known in the West as Koxinga), built up a sizable piratical empire that controlled much of the trade in the South China Sea for some fifty years. Zheng Zhilong, who began his career as a merchant-pirate, displayed remarkable organizational skills and an uncanny knack for manipulating officials. In 1628 he surrendered to the Ming government in exchange for an admiral's commission, and in 1646 he surrendered to the new Qing dynasty (1644–1911), but instead of being rewarded this time he was arrested and finally executed in 1661 (Doc. 15). After his father surrendered to the alien Manchus, Zheng Chenggong rose up in revolt in the name of Ming loyalism. Taking advantage of the political turmoil, he expanded his power base in South China and by 1651 was in command of the Zheng family organization. For the next ten years his fleets monopolized shipping in Fujian, Guangdong, Taiwan, the Philippines, and much of Southeast Asia. He financed his huge maritime syndicate through trade, robbery, and extortion. In 1661, after he failed to take Nanjing, Zheng Chenggong withdrew to Taiwan, where he drove the Dutch away. After his unexpected death six months later, his heirs continued to resist the Manchus until the new dynasty seized Taiwan in 1683.

In the meantime, after the Ming dynasty collapsed, anarchy quickly spread everywhere and piracy escalated out of control. The Qing rulers responded with even harsher sea bans than their predecessors. Between 1661 and 1662, the government adopted a scorched earth policy, forcing residents along the coast to relocate inland at a distance of ten to twenty miles. All houses and property within that no-man's zone were destroyed and anyone caught trying to return to the coast was beheaded. Such draconian measures drove many people who depended on the sea for their livelihood into open rebellion. In the Canton region, in 1663 and 1664, for example, Zhou Yu and Li Rong led bands of displaced fishermen in a pirate uprising that shook the economic core of the province. The actions of such rebel-pirates were motivated less by Ming loyalism than by survival instincts in the face of the harsh government policies.

Already long before the 1660s, the Dutch and British had replaced the Portuguese as the dominant Western powers in Asia, and like their predecessors they also combined trade with piracy. Their main objective was to disrupt the Chinese junk trade with Spanish-controlled Manila. Encouraged by their sovereigns, Dutch and British adventurers took advantage of the political vacuum in China to plunder Chinese junks and coastal towns. The smaller, poorly armed junks provided easy prey for these Western predators. In 1622 the Dutch attacked Macao and then seized the Pescadores, looting and burning villages and kidnapping hundreds of people to sell into slavery. In 1624 they occupied Taiwan, and from this base conducted trade and pirate expeditions until Zheng Chenggong expelled them in 1661. The Dutch, who were excluded from direct trade with China until 1729, actually obtained much of the silks and chinaware so vital to their trade with Japan through plunder. European freebooters continued to seize Chinese and other vessels in the South China Sea into the early eighteenth century.

Between 1680 and 1730, attitudes and public policies toward piracy and trade had changed dramatically in both China and the West. In 1684, just one year after the Qing military had crushed the remnants of Zheng's heirs on Taiwan and had finally secured control over all of China, the Kangxi Emperor (r. 1662–1722) rescinded nearly all of the sea bans. Now convinced that national security depended on the prosperity and stability of the southern coastal provinces, the imperial court legalized the overseas junk trade and opened up several ports to foreign commerce. In the 1720s the Qing government also began enacting a series of laws to protect private property, including harsh new laws against piracy. As the economy quickly recovered, expanded, and prospered, piracy diminished. Chinese merchants, who now had a vested interest in maintaining the existing system, became bulwarks of support in pirate suppression. It was also about the same time that Western merchants began putting pressure on their home governments to suppress piracy. Officials responded by passing tough anti-piracy laws and by building navies to protect their merchant ships on the high seas. Western piracy soon waned in Asia as it did elsewhere around the globe.

The High Tide of Chinese Piracy, 1780–1810

The next great pirate wave, in the late eighteenth and early nineteenth centuries, was an age of indigenous piracy throughout Asia. From the Malabar coast to the Malay Archipelago to the South China Sea, piracy was once again on the rise. The expansion of commerce and resulting prosperity throughout the entire region acted as a catalyst for maritime predation among the poverty-stricken fishermen and sailors living in South China. This was an "age of prosperity," but one in which wealth was unevenly distributed. Despite the flourishing economy, population pressure intensified competition and kept wages low for most seafarers. It is hardly surprising that the majority of pirates in this era were common sailors and fishermen who engaged in occasional piracy in order to survive in an increasingly harsh and competitive world (Doc. 16). Between 1780 and 1810, South China was infested with numerous competing pirate associations, composed of self-contained fleets that functioned independently of one another. Throughout those years, petty gangs of local pirates continued to operate in the shadows of the larger, well-organized fleets of "barbarian pirates" (*yifei*) and "ocean bandits" (*yangdao*).

Large-scale piracy in South China reappeared in the 1780s, when Tâyson rebels in Vietnam began to foster raids into Chinese waters. As a means of obtaining revenue, the rebels, who needed both money and men for their cause, actively recruited Chinese pirates, guaranteed them safe harbors, supplied them with ships and weapons, and rewarded them with official ranks and titles. Because of their Vietnamese sponsorship Chinese officials labeled them "barbarian pirates," though in fact most gangs were Chinese. Pirate fleets set out every spring and summer from bases along the Sino-Vietnamese border for Chinese waters, and returned each autumn laden with booty that they shared with their Tâyson patrons.

Although the pirates had scored great successes in Chinese waters, by 1801 Tâyson power had waned. As the rebel defeat became imminent, thousands of pirates surrendered to Qing officials in return for pardons. Royalist troops also apprehended large numbers of pirates and turned them over to Chinese authorities for execution. The next year royalists had captured the Tâyson pretender and sent the remaining pirates fleeing to China. At first the pirates were in disarray and fighting among themselves, but over the next few years several capable chiefs—particularly Cai Qian and Zheng Yi—began reorganizing the pirates into huge leagues of "ocean bandits."

From bases in Fujian, between 1800 and 1804, Cai Qian slowly came to dominate the entire region between Taiwan and Zhejiang. His wife, known to us only as Matron Cai Qian (Cai Qian Ma), played an important role in his rise to power, reportedly commanding her own fleet of women pirates (Doc. 17). As Cai Qian's power increased so did his activities and his ambitions. His organization grew larger and more powerful through a formalized protection racket that had connections with secret societies on shore (Doc. 18). At the height of his strength, between 1805 and 1806, he made repeated attacks on Taiwan, intent on occupying the island as his base. His forces, however, were defeated in 1806 in a series of battles with the Qing military and local militia. Forced to abandon thousands of comrades on Taiwan, Cai Qian slipped back to Fujian. After purchasing new ships and supplies, he continued for the next several years with forays around Taiwan and Zhejiang, constantly being harassed by the imperial navy. Over the next several years provincial leaders imposed a strict embargo that severed Cai's support on land. In desperation he fled to Vietnam to recuperate, but after returning to China he drowned in a naval battle in October 1809. Without their gallant leader the remnants of his tattered organization soon scattered.

Meanwhile to the south in Guangdong province, once the Tâyson rebels had been defeated in 1802 a pirate chief named Zheng Yi, who came from a long line of Cantonese pirates, began reorganizing the disparate gangs into a huge confederation. In 1805 he led seven of the most powerful pirate leaders in signing a pact intended to impose law and order over the unruly pirates (Doc. 19). The reinvigorated pirates established new bases along Guangdong's coast and outer islands, and soon extended their hegemony over most of the fishing and coastal trade, as well as over many villages and market towns, through a formal protection racket based on extortion, bribery, and terrorism. Even the state-licensed salt trade had fallen victim to the pirates, whose junks had to purchase "safe conduct passes" at two hundred dollars per vessel. The ransom and sale of captives was another major source of pirate income (Doc. 20). Pirates not only built strongholds around such commercial and political hubs as Canton and Macao, but also defiantly established "tax bureaus" inside those cities to collect protection and ransom payments.

In 1807 Zheng Yi died in a storm at sea. The leadership passed into the hands of his widow, Zheng Yi Sao (Wife of Zheng Yi) and the young and ambitious Zhang Bao. Under their combined leadership Guangdong pirates reached the apex of their power. Zheng Yi Sao had been a prostitute on one of Canton's floating brothels before she married Zheng Yi in 1801. She played a key role in helping her husband consolidate his dominance over the burgeoning pirate league. When her husband suddenly died she maneuvered quickly to assure support from the Zheng family in her own bid for power. In taking command she was assisted by the twenty-one year old Zhang Bao, her husband's adopted son and now her lover. Zhang Bao had joined the pirates when he was fifteen, after being kidnapped by Zheng Yi's gang. The young lad quickly came to the attention of the chief, who adopted him into the Zheng family after a homosexual liaison, a common method of initiating adolescents into a gang and of male bonding. In a short time Zhang Bao was given command of his own vessel where he ably demonstrated his skills in both seamanship and piracy. Within weeks of Zheng Yi's death, he was at the side of Zheng Yi Sao, sharing her boudoir and all the power. By that time the confederation had stabilized at six large fleets, each flying a separate colored banner; the pirates now numbered anywhere from 40,000 to 60,000 men.

The Guangdong pirates were at the height of their power in 1809, yet within a year they utterly collapsed. Having repeatedly defeated the imperial navy, the pirates had virtual control over the Guangdong coast and even many inland villages and towns. That summer pirates swarmed deep into the Canton Delta, penetrating within a few miles of Canton itself. A number of Western vessels also came under pirate attack and, in September, Richard Glasspoole was kidnapped for ransom (Doc. 21). Unable to stop the pirates militarily, the emperor initiated a pacification policy, coaxing pirates to surrender in exchange for pardons and rewards. Pirates began to petition to surrender (Doc. 22), and in April 1810, Zhang Bao and Zheng Yi Sao surrendered with over 17,000 followers. The government quickly rewarded Zhang Bao with a naval commission and sent him to fight the remaining pirates, whose resistance quickly crumbled. For all practical purposes the golden age of piracy in China had come to an end, though piracy never completely disappeared in the region.

What was the nature of Chinese piracy, particularly in light of piracy elsewhere in the world? In the sixteenth and seventeenth centuries piracy flourished as never before all around the globe, as it became incorporated into world politics and the emerging world economy. At that time several European states, particularly England, France, and Holland, backed maritime raiding to advance economic development and state-building. Western piracy became global in scope. Likewise, on the Barbary coast corsairing was a state-sponsored activity and essential to the economy. In contrast, no Chinese dynasty ever officially sanctioned piracy as state policy; however, the Ming and early Qing governments adopted such strong anti-commercial policies that many sea merchants were forced into piracy. Though for different reasons, commerce and piracy became indistinguishable in both east and west, and merchants came to play key roles in Chinese, Barbary, and Western piracy. During those years, in all three regions large pirate syndicates were organized as business ventures.

By the early eighteenth century, however, the nature of piracy had changed at both ends of the Eurasian continent. As governments and economies stabilized in China and Europe, and as the profits from legitimate trade grew, merchants increasingly turned away from piracy as a means of trade and instead became bulwarks of support in pirate suppression. Although Western piracy rapidly declined after 1730, it flourished for another century in both Barbary and China. In fact, in China it reached new peaks between 1780 and 1810, as profound demographic and economic changes pushed tens of thousands of poor, marginalized seafarers into piracy as a means of survival. For many of them piracy was a seasonal or occasional occupation, and a necessary supplement to otherwise legitimate pursuits.

Finally, Chinese pirates differed in other important respects from their counterparts elsewhere in the world. Unlike both Mediterranean and Western piracy, Chinese piracy never became entangled in religious conflicts. Although they were outlaws living by their own rules, Chinese pirates did not exhibit the same sorts of democratic and egalitarian ideals found among Western pirates (as described by Marcus Rediker in Part 3). There was no collective authority in the hands of the crew aboard Chinese pirate ships. The captains were not democratically elected but ruled their ships autocratically. They made all the rules and composed codes not to guarantee the liberty of gang members but to ensure order and discipline. In South China, because many women worked and lived aboard ships, it was not unusual to find females among the pirates. Unlike the women aboard Western pirate ships, however, Chinese women did not have to disguise themselves as men. (See Jo Stanley's essay in Part 3.) Instead, they lived and worked openly as pirates. Women were not merely tolerated by their male shipmates but, as the cases of Cai Qian Ma and Zheng Yi Sao show, they were even able to exercise leadership roles aboard their ships.

Raiders, Warriors, and Traders in Southeast Asia

Although the earliest recorded incidents of piracy in Southeast Asia date from the fifth century, it reached its peak between 1750 and 1860, a time long after it had been suppressed in other areas of the world. The region was ideal for pirates—rich and busy trade routes inadequately protected by strong states and navies, a maze of islands crisscrossed by narrow straits that created commercial bottlenecks, and coasts lined with dense mangrove swamps that provided safe havens for outlaws. Besides the European enclaves, the entire region was divided into numerous rival kingdoms and tribal groups, whose incessant warfare assured that no single power dominated the region or its sea lanes. In fact, many local polities actually supported marauding as a means of gaining wealth and power. Piracy kept pace with the expansion of trade and colonization. Numerous indigenous and foreign peoples actively engaged in sea raiding: Muslim Malays, Bugis seafarers, Iranun and Balangingi slavers of Sulu, and Sea Dayak headhunters of Borneo, as well as Chinese, Japanese, and European renegades and outlaws. Piracy, which followed regular annual cycles according to the rhythms of monsoons and commerce, was an integral part of the social, political, and economic life of Southeast Asia.

Yet before the appearance of Europeans in Southeast Asia, Western notions of piracy were unknown in the region. Indeed, the terms pirate and piracy were European constructs that came with colonization. (See Campo's essay in Part 3.) Fundamentally, for Western merchants and officials anyone who operated outside the colonial trading system or who opposed them was a pirate. In the sixteenth and seventeenth centuries, the Portuguese and Dutch, who attempted to monopolize the spice trade, believed it their right and duty to suppress as pirates both indigenous and foreign inter- lopers. Piracy frequently was used as an excuse for intervention and extension of European power and culture in Southeast Asia. The suppression of piracy was a crusading and civilizing mission intri- cately entwined with colonialism.

For Europeans, the term "piracy" carried connotations that would have been foreign to natives of Southeast Asia. For many of them raiding was a way of life closely tied to war, slavery, and trade. Throughout the region intertribal warfare was an important aspect of society and warfare was related to maritime raiding. While viewed as criminal acts by Europeans, raiding was actually a respectable profession pursued not only by individuals but by entire communities and even kingdoms. It was a common means for war- riors and chiefs to increase their power and prestige. Unlike in China or the West, maritime raiding did not necessarily involve criminality or rebellion against society. Raiders were not antisocial dissidents living on the fringes of society. Rather, they were respectable members of their communities and, in fact, many were popular heroes, admired for their courage and moral fortitude (Doc. 23). Piracy enabled communities to work outside colonial administrative jurisdictions and patterns of trade, thereby allowing them a degree of independence. In this area of the world, it has been suggested that piracy was a type of trade based on theft rather than exchange.

In this section we will explore the various forms and patterns of "piracy" between 1520 and 1860 in Southeast Asia. Although Western pirates occasionally made their way into Southeast Asian waters, they never posed as much of a threat to the prosperity and stability of the area as the buccaneers had done in the Caribbean. Their presence virtually disappeared in the archipelagoes by the early eighteenth century. Chinese and Japanese pirates also sporad- ically infiltrated the area during the entire period, and indigenous forms of piracy or maritime raiding actually expanded throughout the whole region during the eighteenth and early nineteenth centuries.

Western Pirates in Southeast Asia, 1570–1700

In the late sixteenth century, European explorers began to make expeditions to the Orient and in their wake came outlaws, renegades, and adventurers. Soon afterward they were joined by Western pirates, some working out of their home countries or American colonies, while others operated from bases in the Indian Ocean and elsewhere in Asia. Many others, often deserters and runaways from the burgeoning colonial service, went native and joined forces with indigenous sea raiders in Southeast Asia. They routinely served as gunners, pilots, and even as commanders on Asian vessels. These explorers, renegades, and pirates left an indelible mark on the maritime history of the East in the early modern era.

Francis Drake entered the Pacific Ocean in 1577 as an interloper and a pirate. At the time virtually the entire Pacific had been claimed by the Spanish, while the Portuguese had claimed the Indian Ocean and much of Southeast Asia as its own. Yet neither country was ever strong enough to keep others out. Drake was the first Englishman to cross the Pacific and to challenge the Iberians. His voyage clearly showed that the riches of the East were at the mercy of anyone daring and able enough to take them. Although his motives for crossing the Pacific remain unclear, plunder was undoubtedly on his mind. The *Golden Hind* was a floating arsenal, armed well beyond the needs for carrying on peaceful trade (see Doc. 2). While most of his loot had been taken from Spanish ships and settlements on the Pacific coast of America, after his unfriendly encounter with natives in 1579 on the "Island of Thieves," Drake continued to the Philippines and while in the Celebes Sea he attempted unsuccessfully to rob a Portuguese trading vessel. In the Spice Islands (Moluccas), Drake tried to cheat the Sultan of Ternate out of his duty on six tons of cloves, although he ultimately paid for them with silver he had stolen from the Spanish. Drake returned to London in 1580 with a boatload of (mostly stolen) goods—silver, gold, jewels, and cloves worth perhaps £600,000, and it is estimated that he earned for his investors a staggering

4,700 percent profit. The queen, too, likely received a share valued at £300,000, an amount exceeding a year's Exchequer receipts. And this was at a time when England was nominally at peace with Spain and Portugal.

Drake was not alone. Throughout the late sixteenth and seventeenth centuries, European pirates and privateers continually pillaged Southeast Asia. During the first half of the seventeenth century, Spanish, Dutch, English, French, and even Danish rovers repeatedly robbed indigenous, Chinese, and Japanese trading vessels around Sumatra, Java, and the Malay Peninsula. By the end of the century, European pirates, often in cooperation with local gangs, were regularly capturing Chinese junks in the Straits of Malacca and plundering Western merchant ships bound for Japan or Manila in the South China Sea. During the 1680s the buccaneer William Dampier was aboard several pirate ships that robbed Spanish and Portuguese vessels between Manila and Malacca. In 1683 the English freebooter Samuel White had organized a fleet of native craft, sanctioned by the king of Siam, to pillage shipping in the Bay of Bengal and off the coast of Acheh. In 1696 Robert Culliford sailed out of Madagascar to plunder his way across the Indian Ocean to the Straits of Malacca.

After 1700 the number of Western pirates, apart from those who had gone native, had greatly decreased. The effects of European suppression campaigns were being felt even in the far corners of Southeast Asia. Piracy was replaced with privateering as wars continued in Europe and overseas. As was the case in the Caribbean, the on-and-off conflicts among the European powers in the sixteenth to eighteenth centuries made firm distinctions between piracy, privateering, and outright warfare problematical in Southeast Asian waters.

Chinese and Japanese Pirates in Southeast Asia, 1520–1860

The situation in Southeast Asia was further complicated by the persistent presence of Chinese and occasionally Japanese pirates in the region over the entire period. They came in three waves. The first, lasting from 1520 to 1650, was a time of sporadic raids by

Chinese and Japanese pirates, who combined trade with piracy. The second wave peaked in the last two decades of the eighteenth century, when Chinese pirates joined forces with Tâyson rebels in Vietnam to conduct regular raids in Chinese and Southeast Asian waters. This was followed by a period of intermittent forays that continued until the start of the third wave of Chinese pirate activity in Southeast Asia, which lasted from the 1830s through the 1850s.

The sixteenth and early seventeenth centuries were a time of change and instability not only in the West but also in Asia. As noted previously, in China the Ming Dynasty pursued a rigid closed-door policy that criminalized sea merchants, and at the end of the century the country was mired in a destructive dynastic war that lasted until 1684, when the Manchus finally consolidated their authority over all of China. During much of this same period, Japan was embroiled in a century-long civil war that ended with the establishment of the Tokugawa Shogunate in 1603. Under these conditions, disgruntled Chinese merchants and masterless Japanese warriors took to the sea as pirates (Doc. 14). In the mid-sixteenth century, members of the wealthy Xu family in China, who were involved in the Malacca trade and had Malaccan wives, turned to smuggling and piracy when the Ming government imposed strict prohibitions on overseas trade. Xu Dong cooperated with Japanese and Portuguese adventurers on combined trading and raiding ventures in Southeast Asia. After his execution in 1548, his subordinate, Wang Zhi, continued the illicit operations on the China coast and in Thailand, until he was beheaded eleven years later. Another Chinese pirate, Lin Feng, operated from a stronghold on Taiwan to plunder shipping in the South China Sea during the 1570s. In 1574 he commanded a fleet of over thirty junks which pillaged towns and challenged Spanish authority in the Philippines for nearly a year. Also between 1580 and 1582, the Spanish reported Japanese pirates who repeatedly harassed the area from bases on Luzon itself. Then, in the turbulent first quarter of the seventeenth century, Zheng Zhilong and his son, Zheng Chenggong (Koxinga), established a piratical empire that encompassed the whole South China Sea. From bases, first on Amoy and later on Taiwan, they carried on a triangular trade mixed with piracy and extortion in

China, Japan, and Southeast Asia. It was said that all ships sailing in this wide zone were liable to attack unless they paid tribute to the Zheng syndicate (see Doc. 15). Only the death of Zheng Chenggong in 1662 saved the Philippines from attack after the Spanish authorities had refused him tribute.

In the 1780s and 1790s, Chinese pirates cooperated with Tâyson rebels on regular seasonal raids along the coast from Wenzhou in South China to Saigon in South Vietnam. Following the monsoons, each year in the spring pirates would set off from their bases at Giang Binh and on Hainan Island on the Sino-Vietnamese frontier to plunder towns and shipping on the China coast, and then after returning to their bases and refitting in the autumn they would set sail for raids along the coasts of Vietnam and Gulf of Siam (Map 5). In the late 1790s, Chinese pirates, who occasionally allied with Bugis raiders, extended their activities to the Sunda Strait, where they robbed Dutch and native trading ships. Even after the Tâyson Rebellion was crushed in 1802, Chinese pirates continued their excursions on the Vietnamese coast and Philippine Islands until the huge pirate leagues in South China were defeated in 1810.

After a lull of several years, a final surge of Chinese piracy in Southeast Asia began in the 1830s and lasted until the late 1850s. The disturbances of the Opium War (1839–42) followed by the suppression campaigns of British warships in the 1840s and 1850s around Hong Kong drove many Chinese pirates into Southeast Asia. Between 1839 and 1849, the *Dai Nam Thuc Luc* (*Veritable Record of Vietnam*) recorded over forty separate incidents of Chinese pirates plundering towns and ships on the Vietnamese coast. Most of these pirates followed the same seasonal patterns as the earlier marauders— leaving bases on the Sino-Vietnamese border in the fall to plunder the south. In many cases, too, pirates continued to call at British Hong Kong to sell their loot and recruit gangs (Doc. 24). Not only Vietnam but also the whole Malay Archipelago suffered from the resurgence in Chinese piracy at this time. Although pirates sometimes attacked Western merchant ships, their chief targets were the smaller and poorly armed native trading vessels. Chinese piracy became such a huge problem that it disrupted foreign trade at the great emporiums of Singapore and Batavia. Yet, as in Hong Kong,

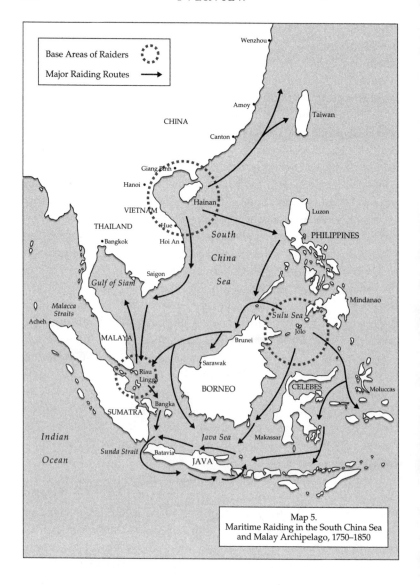

Map 5.
Maritime Raiding in the South China Sea
and Malay Archipelago, 1750–1850

merchants in Singapore and on many of the surrounding islands continued to outfit pirates despite the attempts at suppression. It was not until the early 1860s that Chinese piracy in the whole region was brought under control.

Indigenous Piracy in Southeast Asia, 1520–1860

According to Francis Drake the inhabitants of his Island of Thieves—most likely Palau or Yap in the Eastern Caroline Islands—were unrelenting and incorrigible larcenists. While they brought out trifles on pretense of honest trade, their true intentions (said Drake) were to steal whatever they got their hands on: "for if they received anything once into their hands, they would neither give recompence nor restitution of it, but thought whatever they could finger to bee their owne." Successive waves of natives came out in canoes to the *Golden Hind* and when Drake and his men rejected their supplications, the islanders hurled stones at the foreigners. To rid his ship of these unwelcome visitors Drake fired his guns, killing perhaps twenty natives (Doc. 25). Other European explorers had similar experiences in the Western Pacific and Malay Archipelago. Even before Drake was born, in 1521, Ferdinand Magellan happened upon another group of islands that he called the Ladrones or the "Pirate Islands,"[14] which make up the Marianas, after the natives stole one of his boats. On another island, wrote Antonio Pigafetta, "the inhabitants . . . entered the ships and stole whatever they could lay hands on, so that we could not protect ourselves."[15] Later, Borneo natives kidnapped members of Magellan's crew. Likewise when other Spanish explorers visited Mindanao, in the southern Philippines, they found the natives to be devious and treacherous, earning one small cove on the island's southern tip the name "Deceitful Bay."

What are we to make of these native pirates? As William Lessa explained, "The aggressive and thieving actions of the islanders were not the result of a sudden transformation of character brought on by the foreigners."[16] Robbery and violence had existed long before the Europeans had arrived, and were, in fact, closely related to the endless intertribal wars among the islanders. Treachery, deceit, and thievery were all instruments of political policy.

[14] One of the Ladrones was the island of Guam, which throughout the age of sail served as a favorite rendezvous for both pirates and traders voyaging across the Pacific.

[15] Cited in William A. Lessa, *Drake's Island of Thieves: Ethnological Sleuthing* (Honolulu: University Press of Hawaii, 1975), p. 117.

[16] *Ibid.*, p. 254.

Chiefs, kings, and sultans organized forces of maritime warriors and they also allied with sea raiders, whom they relied upon to rob and debilitate their enemies. Maritime marauding was one of the key strategies used by political leaders to expand their prestige, wealth, and power. The seizure of scarce and valuable resources, particularly slaves and weapons, was a major motive for wars. The accumulation of slaves, not territorial aggrandizement, was the basis of political power and wealth; warriors needed weapons for slave raids. Under such conditions, distinctions between warfare and piracy became meaningless (see Doc. 23).

The dynamics of indigenous piracy or sea raiding changed dramatically in the second half of the eighteenth century, as did the number of incidents. Piracy surged at a time of economic vitality across the whole region as Southeast Asia was drawn into the emerging global economy. Raiding became closely tied to the nascent China trade, as well as to European expansion and colonialism. As the Chinese economy grew so too did the demand in China for Southeast Asian products, especially culinary exotics like birds' nests, sharks' fins, and sea cucumbers, as well as for pepper, pearls, tortoise shells, and tin. European traders also actively sought these same local products to trade in China. Because there was always a shortage of laborers to procure these products, slave raiding became a big business. The increasing need for slaves perpetuated raiding and war. Piracy went virtually unchecked for nearly a century between 1750 and 1840, not only because many native polities fostered raiding, but also because European governments were occupied with problems back home, particularly the Napoleonic Wars (1799–1815), as well as with commercial rivalries.

In the late eighteenth century the Sulu Archipelago was the center for Southeast Asian sea raiding. Iranun and Balangingi raiders, and their Tausog overlords, created a highly organized, large-scale operation which by the early nineteenth century extended throughout insular Southeast Asia and to the shores of Thailand and South Vietnam. Sulu sultans and *datus* (chiefs or nobles) supported raiders for a percentage of the booty. Cruises were annual undertakings: in the winter during the northeast monsoons raiders set sail from their Sulu bases for the Celebes, Borneo, Java, Sumatra, and Malacca, and in the autumn they returned home with the southeast

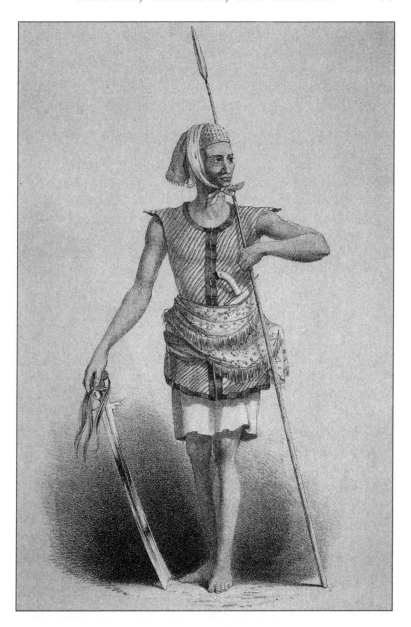

FIGURE 6
Iranun Sea Raider (David Cordingly, ed., *Pirates*, 1996.)

monsoons (Map 5). In 1798 one fleet, which consisted of twenty-five ships with 500 fighters and 800 rowers, captured 450 people who were sold into slavery; included among the captives were three Spanish priests, one of whom was sold for 2,500 pesos.

Captives, who were sold or bartered as slaves, were the chief source of booty as well as of regional trade. They were important to the economy both as a unit of production and as a commodity of exchange. Jolo, called the "Algiers of the East," became the largest slave market in the region and the hub for long-distance slave raiding. Between 1770 and 1870, an estimated 300,000 slaves were trafficked by raiders in Sulu. While many slaves were put to work harvesting, procuring, and processing jungle and marine products for the China market, others worked as agricultural and domestic laborers. A large number of captives were simply traded as commodities in areas outside the Sulu Archipelago, while others were retained by the raiders as oarsmen (Doc. 26). Elderly and infirm captives often were sold to headhunters in Borneo for human sacrifice. Jolo was an open market where European, Chinese, and Bugis merchants came to trade, and where raiders could sell booty and refit their ships. Trading and raiding overlapped and complemented one another.

Another important raiding base was centered around Singapore on the islands of Riau, Galang, and Lingga, areas that were the traditional core of the Kingdom of Johor (Map 5). Piracy was as ancient in this area as elsewhere in the region, and was pursued for many of the same reasons, namely war, slavery, and trade. Groups of Malay Muslims, called the Orang Laut or Sea Gypsies, were nomadic seafarers who spent most of their time on ceaseless trading and raiding expeditions throughout the archipelagos. In the nineteenth century, Iranun raiders also cooperated with Malay pirates and used Lingga as a forward base for interregional raiding operations (Doc. 27). They not only abducted people for slavery, but also plundered trading vessels, which carried valuable cargoes of marine products, pepper, and weapons. From the 1760s onward there emerged an intricate clandestine trading network, which involved raiders and merchants. Booty was brought to the markets at Riau, Lingga, and later, after its founding in 1819, Singapore, where Western and Chinese traders exchanged foreign commodities—textiles and opium from India and ceramics from China—for stolen goods. The illegal trade became so important and lucrative that in 1782, at a time when the Dutch claimed a monopoly on all trade in the region, English merchants actually provided a vessel to raiders so that they could plunder ships carrying pepper in the Sunda Strait.

Piracy surged in the region between 1784 and 1836. For the Orang Laut and other sea peoples in Johor this was a time of crisis following the Dutch invasion of Riau (1784), and the establishment of British settlements at Penang (1786), Malacca (1795), and Singapore (1819). Adding further to the general crisis was the almost constant warfare between Bugis and Malays. In this anarchy, native trading vessels suffered the most. As rivalries and conflicts intensified so too did the wanton brutality. In response to Western imperialism and hostility the number of attacks on Western vessels likewise increased. Cruelty toward Western sailors could be horrendous, as the case of William Edwards demonstrates (Doc. 28). The disturbances became particularly worrisome to Europeans in Singapore who feared continued attacks on native and European shipping would destroy the commerce of the port.

Most Westerners treated indigenous wars and raiding simply as piracy and activities that had to be suppressed for the sake of commerce and civilization. They considered raiding a common and barbaric custom among the natives of Southeast Asia. According to one writer, the Malays were "barbarous and poor, therefore rapacious, faithless, and sanguinary. These are circumstances . . . which militate strongly to beget a piratical character."[17] On the one hand, natives had to be encouraged to adopt the "industrious habits" of the West, and on the other hand, Western navies had to implement aggressive campaigns against the pirates and their supporters. The natives, it seems, had to be saved from themselves. Beginning in 1836, the British and other European powers began to adopt effective piracy-suppression measures around Singapore and elsewhere in Southeast Asia. Perhaps the most effective measure was the deployment of steam gunboats to the region and their relentless destruction of pirate vessels and strongholds. Subdued pirate communities were also forcefully resettled in new areas away from their original power bases, where they were expected to engage in the

[17] "The Piracy and Slave Trade of the Indian Archipelago," *Journal of the Indian Archipelago and Eastern Asia* 4 (1850): 45.

legitimate pursuits of agriculture and trade. By 1860 their campaigns had become so successful that piracy ceased being a serious problem in Southeast Asia for the next century.

In Southeast Asia, as elsewhere, men became pirates and raiders for many reasons—poverty, debt, hunger, and greed. Although many of the raiders themselves were poor, their leaders were normally men of wealth and power. As with Mediterranean corsairing and Elizabethan piracy, sea raiding in Southeast Asia was regarded as a legitimate and honorable pursuit. Here too raiding was a state-sponsored enterprise and deeply entwined with trade, war, and slavery. Only gradually and grudgingly did indigenous states come to accept Western notions that "piracy" was a crime that needed to be eliminated. As a legal concept and a cultural construct imposed by Western colonialists, piracy in any form became a stigma of backwardness and savagery; its suppression therefore became an important and necessary component of modernization.

Global Piracy Today

Piracy is as old as the first ships. While maritime raiding reached a zenith during the late seventeenth and early eighteenth centuries in the West, its heyday in the South China Sea extended into the next century. By the 1860s, however, piracy apparently had disappeared from most areas of the world. After a long lull there has been a resurgence in recent years. Today piracy appears in many of the same areas where it had been rampant a hundred or two hundred years ago: along the coasts of Malaysia, Indonesia, and the Philippines; on the Sino-Vietnamese border; on the west coast of South America and in parts of the Caribbean; at the mouth of the Red Sea; and along the coasts of East and West Africa. The struggle to eliminate piracy remains a persistent problem. According to data collected by the International Maritime Bureau (IMB), in 1998 there were over two hundred reported cases of piracy worldwide, and in the following year there were over three hundred incidents. In 2003 the IMB reported that pirate attacks on ships had tripled over the previous decade, with over a hundred attacks in just the first three months of the year. Today piracy and marine fraud is a $16-billion business.

Piracy has always thrived in areas where the rewards were great and the risks were slight, and where pirates could find protection and support. Predators like Drake and Morgan found the heavily laden Spanish treasure galleons easy targets, and today small speedboats easily overtake slow-moving and unarmed tankers. Today, as in the past, many of the best hunting grounds are those areas where governments are weak or are handicapped by international rivalries. Thus piracy has usually flourished in developing areas where the authorities were unable or unwilling to intervene, or where governments offered raiders protection and support. Currently one of the most dangerous areas is the Straits of Malacca, traversed by over 50,000 ships each year. The nearby islands of the Malay Archipelago provide ideal hiding places and friendly ports for pirates just as they have for centuries.

While many of the favorite pirate haunts are the same as in the past, pirate *modi operandi* have changed. Sailing vessels have given

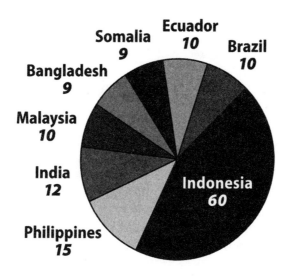

FIGURE 7

Worldwide Pirate Attacks, 1998 (www.cargolaw.com/presentations_pirates. html. Accessed March 2006.)

way to motorized craft and speedboats and crews are armed with automatic weapons and modern navigational equipment. Today's petty pirates engage in mostly short-distance, hit-and-run attacks inside congested harbors where they sneak aboard anchored vessels to steal whatever they can get their hands on. Their attacks are generally random and disorganized, and heists consist chiefly of cash, personal belongings, and sundry other items valued at no more than several thousand dollars. Professional pirates operate on a long-term basis and are well organized, sometimes having links to larger criminal and drug syndicates. They bribe local officials for protection and access to markets. In some cases they have connections to political insurgents and terrorists, providing them with financial support in exchange for aid. After seizing ships, they dispose of the crews, sell the cargo, and use the vessels to commit further crimes. In November 1998, pirates dressed as Chinese officials seized the *Cheung Son* near Hong Kong and threw the 23-man crew overboard to drown. Later Chinese police arrested 38 men, sentencing thirteen to death for piracy. In June 2002, pirates boarded an oil tanker in Thai waters, threw the crew overboard and sailed away. The crew members were rescued by Indonesian fishermen, and the vessel was later found—with a new paint job and a new name—docked in the area with its cargo missing.

While piracy today seems clear-cut and well-defined in international law, in fact it is as murky as ever. Governments that decry piracy as a serious crime in some cases turn a blind eye to the perpetrators or refuse to prosecute them. Those people labeled as pirates often perceive themselves and their actions differently. Some see themselves as modern-day Robin Hoods and others as freedom fighters, not as pirates or terrorists. What the eighteenth-century pirate Samuel Bellamy supposedly told to his prisoner Captain Beer still holds true today: "... *damn ye, you are a sneaking Puppy, and so are all those who will submit to be governed by Laws which rich Men have made for their own Security.* ... *They villify us, the Scoundrels do, when there is only this Difference, they rob the Poor under the Cover of Law, forsooth, and we plunder the Rich under the Protection of our own Courage.* ..."[18]

---

[18] Charles Johnson, *The History of the Pyrates*, 2 vols. (London, 1728), II, p. 220.

II

Documents

Pirates of the West

Doc. 1: *Captain Plowman's Privateering Commission, 1703*

During times of war European governments frequently issued commissions to private individuals allowing them to attack the vessels of their enemies. The following document, issued during Queen Anne's War (1702–13), was a privateering license from the governor of colonial Massachusetts, which permitted Capt. Plowman to attack and destroy all vessels of France and Spain during the time of war with England.

Joseph Dudley, Esq; Captain General and Governour in Chief, in and over Her Majesties Provinces of the Massachusetts Bay, *and* New-Hampshire *in* New-England *in* America, *and Vice-Admiral of the same. To Capt.* Daniel Plowman, *Commander of the Briganteen* Charles *of Boston, Greeting.*

WHEREAS Her Sacred Majesty *ANNE* by the Grace of GOD, of *England, Scotland, France* and *Ireland,* QUEEN, Defender of the Faith, Etc. Hath an Open and Declared War against *France* and *Spain,* their Vassals and Subjects. And FORASMUCH as you have made Application unto Me for Licence to Arm, Furnish and Equip the said Briganteen in Warlike manner, against Her Majesties said Enemies, I do accordingly Permit and Allow the same; And, Reposing special Trust and Confidence in your Loyalty, Courage and good Conduct, Do by these Presents, by Virtue of the Powers and Authorities contained in Her Majesties Royal Commission to Me granted, Impower and Commissionate you the said *Daniel Plowman*, to be Captain or Commander of the said Briganteen *Charles*, Burthen Eighty Tuns or thereabouts: Hereby Authorizing you in and with the said Briganteen and Company to her belonging, to War, Fight, Take, Kill, Suppress and Destroy, any Pirates, Privateers, or other the Subjects and Vassals of *France*, or *Spain*, the Declared Enemies of the Crown of *England*, in what Place soever you shall happen to meet them; Their Ships, Vessels and Goods, to take and make Prize of. And your said Briganteens Company are Commanded to Obey you as their Captain: And your self in the Execution of this Commission, to Observe and Follow the Orders and Instructions[1] herewith given you. And I do hereby Request all Governors and Commanders in Chief, of any of Her Majesties Territories, Islands, Provinces or Plantations, where the said Captain or Commander shall arrive with his said Vessel and Men: And all Admirals, Vice-Admirals and Commanders of Her Majesties Ships of War, and others, that may happen to meet him at Sea; Also all Officers and Subjects of the Friends or Allies of Her said Sacred Majesty, to permit him the said Captain or Commander with his said Vessel, Men, and the Prizes that he may have taken, freely and quietly to pass and repass, without giving or suffering him to receive any Trouble or Hindrance, but on the contrary all Succour and Assistance needful. And this Commission is to continue in Force for the Space of Six Months next ensuing (if the War so long last) and not afterwards. *Given under my Hand and Seal at Arms at* Boston *the Thirteenth Day of* July: *In the Second Year of Her said Majesties Reign,* Annoque Domini, 1703.

   By His Excellencies Command,
   Isaac Addington, Secr.

George Francis Dow and John Henry Edmonds, *The Pirates of the New England Coast, 1630–1730*. Salem: Marine Research Society, 1923, pp. 371–372.

[1] Besides this commission Captain Plowman also received detailed instructions, consisting of ten items, concerning the operation of his privateering vessel.

Doc. 2: *Francis Drake on the Pacific Coast of America, 1579*

Francis Drake was—and still is—a national hero in England, but a mere pirate in Spain. On many occasions he plundered Spanish ships and towns in the West Indies and Pacific coast of America. Was he a pirate or a privateer, a hero or villain? In his attacks on the Spaniards, was he motivated by patriotism, religious zeal, or simply greed? The following two selections come from individuals who had been abducted by Drake. The first is testimony taken from Nuño da Silva, a Portuguese pilot and captain who had been seized by Drake in January 1578 off the west coast of Africa near Cape Verde. Da Silva recounts Drake's pillaging the west coast of Spanish America between February and April, 1579. The second selection is from the testimony of Don Francisco de Zarate, who had been abducted by Drake off the coast of Guatemala in April 1579. He gives a vivid description of Drake's ship, the Golden Hind, *and of Drake as an autocratic commander.*

1. Testimony of Nuño da Silva:

On the 7th of said month [February, 1579] he [Drake] started for the coast and on the 9th went to a port in which he seized another ship which had, however, been unloaded but two hours previously and had carried 800 bars of gold belonging to His Majesty [the king of Spain]; which was great luck. He immediately left that port and went along the coast, leaving behind him all the ships he had taken and coasting with only his vessel and the launch. On the 13th he reached Callao de Lima [Peru] where 19 vessels were lying at anchor. He searched them all and, not finding any silver, cut their cables and the masts of the large vessels. He set sail in pursuit of a ship that had reached the port from Panama, laden with merchandise, and whose crew had gone ashore in a boat. He seized the ship, laden as she was, and took the silks he found in her. Everything else he cast into the sea and he set the ship adrift because two large ships had come out from Lima after her. Taking flight the Englishmen escaped and let her drive.

On the 20th he took a small ship on her way to Lima laden with native products, all of which he threw into the sea, taking from each ship her pilot and releasing the ship. Running along the coast, he reached Arequipa where he found and seized a ship laden with a cargo of Castilian goods. He left this and only took her pilot, being in a hurry to look out for vessels laden with silver.

On * * * the 26th of February, he took another ship bound for Lima from Panama and laden with Castilian wearing apparel. He only took a negro from this ship and let her drive.

He continued his voyage, and on the 27th of February, at night, took another ship bound for Panama and laden with provisions for the King's vessels, with two thousand bags and other things and with 40 bars of silver and gold. And because a sailor secretly took a bar of gold and did not declare it, he hanged him and let the ship go.[1]

Continuing his voyage along the coast, on the night of March 1st he took a ship, in which he found 1300 bars of assayed silver; much silver in small pieces, and much gold, of which there were 300 bars belonging to the King, and 14 chests of reals.[2] He left the ship and did not dare to enter the port of Panama after having captured so good a prize, nor to delay, for fear of the two vessels that had pursued his ship from Lima. He took good care not to enter the town of Panama.

On March 20th, whilst lying at anchor in an isolated port, of which deponent does not know the name nor more than that it was on the coast of Nicaragua, the Englishman took a frigate laden with maize and other native products. On this were two pilots who had been sent by His Excellency from New Spain to Panama. He took one of these pilots and left the other and brought the frigate with him, which is the same one with which he entered this port. On account of contrary weather he was not able to make the port of Realejo, where he intended to anchor.

He continued his voyage and passed by Acaxutlila but did not enter the port, because he saw that there was no vessel therein.

---

[1] This incident actually refers to Francisco Jacome, a ship's clerk, who was "hanged" by Drake to extract information about where treasures were hidden aboard the ship. Although the ordeal was undoubtedly traumatic, Jacome lived to testify to the Spanish authorities. His deposition stated: "As deponent had not hidden anything whatsoever and was unable to reveal anything to them [Drake and his men], they hanged him by the neck with a cord as though to hang him outright, and let him drop from high into the sea, from which they fetched him out with the launch and took him back to the ship on which he had come" (*New Light on Drake* . . . , trans. and ed. Zelia Nuttall [London, 1914], p. 151).

[2] A real was a Spanish coin worth one-eighth of a piece of eight.

On the 4th of April he seized a frigate on which Don Francisco de Zarate was travelling. He brought the frigate with him for two days, at the end of which he took from her twenty-eight half loads of clothing (most of which belonged to two passengers who were travelling in her) and a negress[3] belonging to Don Francisco. Afterwards he released the frigate and her occupants.

2. Testimony of Don Francisco de Zarate:

This general of the Englishmen is a nephew of John Hawkins, and is the same who, about five years ago, took the port of Nombre de Dios. He is called Francisco Drac, and is a man about 35 years of age, low of stature, with a fair beard, and is one of the greatest mariners that sails the seas, both as a navigator and as a commander. His vessel is a galleon of nearly four hundred tons, and is a perfect sailer. She is manned with a hundred men, all of service, and of an age for warfare, and all are as practised therein as old soldiers from Italy could be. Each one takes particular pains to keep his arquebuse[4] clean. He treats them with affection, and they treat him with respect. He carries with him nine or ten cavaliers, cadets of English noblemen. These form a part of his council which he calls together for even the most trivial matter, although he takes advice from no one. But he enjoys hearing what they say and afterwards issues his orders. He has no favourite.

The aforesaid gentlemen sit at his table, as well as a Portuguese pilot, whom he brought from England, who spoke not a word during all the time I was on board.[5] He is served on silver dishes with gold borders and gilded garlands, in which are his arms. He carries all possible dainties and perfumed waters. He said that many of these had been given him by the Queen.

None of these gentlemen took a seat or covered his head before him, until he repeatedly urged him to do so. This galleon of his

---

[3] This female slave, named Maria, became pregnant—some say by Drake—during the long voyage and was later marooned with several other male slaves with some rice, seeds, and the "means for making a fire" on an uninhabited island south of the Celebes.

[4] The arquebuse was a matchlock gun invented in the mid-fifteenth century. The earliest versions were so heavy that they had to be fired using a support. By the end of the next century, they were superseded by the musket.

[5] Zarate is here referring to Nuño da Silva, who had been seized off West Africa, not England.

carries about thirty heavy pieces of artillery and a great quantity of firearms with the requisite ammunition and lead. He dines and sups to the music of viols. He carries trained carpenters and artisans, so as to be able to careen the ship at any time. Beside being new, the ship has a double lining. I understood that all the men he carries with him receive wages, because, when our ship was sacked, no man dared take anything without his orders. He shows them great favour, but punishes the least fault. He also carries painters who paint for him pictures of the coast in its exact colours. This I was most grieved to see, for each thing is so naturally depicted that no one who guides himself according to these paintings can possibly go astray. I understood from him that he had sailed from his country with five vessels, four sloops (of the long kind) and that half of the armada belonged to the Queen.

New Light on Drake: A Collection of Documents Relating to His Voyage of Circumnavigation, 1577–1580. Translated and edited by Zelia Nuttall. London: Hakluyt Society, 1914, pp. 206–208, 248–252.

Doc. 3: *The Manner of the Buccaneers*

The buccaneers of the Caribbean, who called themselves the Brethren of the Coast, lived a free and rugged life on the island fringes of the Spanish Empire. Living in pairs, according to a custom called metelotage, *which implied a sort of same-sex marriage, they spent part of the year hunting wild cattle and pigs and the rest of the year marauding. They gained a reputation as bloodthirsty pirates, but among themselves they lived simple democratic and egalitarian lives. The following selection, taken from the first-hand account of Alexander Exquemelin, depicts the manner of the early buccaneers, with their concerns about procuring meat and sharing out booty in a fair and equitable manner. A number of their habits, including written articles and insuring compensation to wounded comrades, were followed by later pirates (see Doc. 9).*

Before the Pirates go out to sea, they give notice unto every one that goes upon the voyage, of the day on which they ought precisely to embark, intimating also to them their obligation of bringing each man in particular so many pounds of powder and bullets as they think necessary for that expedition. Being all come on board, they join together in council, concerning what place they ought first to go to wherein to get provisions—especially of flesh, seeing they scarce eat anything else. And of this the most common sort among them is pork. The next food is tortoises, which they are accustomed to salt a little. Sometimes they resolve to rob such or such hog-yards, wherein the Spaniards often have a thousand heads of swine together. They come to these places in the dark of the night, and having beset the keeper's lodge, they force him to rise, and give them as many heads as they desire, threatening withal to kill him in case he disobeys their commands or makes any noise. Yea, these menaces are oftentimes put in execution, without giving any quarter to the miserable swine-keepers, or any other person that endcavours to hinder their robberies.

Having got provisions of flesh sufficient for their voyage, they return to their ship. Here their allowance, twice a day to every one, is as much as he can eat, without either weight or measure. Neither does the steward of the vessel give any greater proportion of flesh, or anything else, unto the Captain than to the meanest mariner. The ship being well victualled, they call another council, to deliberate towards what place they shall go to seek their desperate fortunes. In this council, likewise, they agree upon certain articles, which are put in writing, by way of bond or obligation, which every one is bound to observe, and all of them, or the chief, set their hands to it. Herein they specify, and set down very distinctly, what sums of money each particular person ought to have for that voyage, the fund of all the payments being the common stock of what is gotten by the whole expedition; for otherwise it is the same law, among these people as with other Pirates: *No prey, no pay*.[1] In the first place, therefore, they mention how much the Captain ought to have for his ship. Next the salary of the carpenter, or shipwright, who careened, mended, and rigged the vessel. This commonly amounts to one hundred or an hundred and fifty pieces of eight,[2] being, according to the agreement, more or less. Afterwards for

---

[1] Their principle of "no prey, no pay" came from standard privateering traditions, whereby sailors received pay only if they took prizes.

[2] Pieces of eight were Spanish silver coins divided into eight *reales*, which, at the time, were valued at roughly 5 shillings.

provisions and victualling they draw out of the same common stock about two hundred pieces of eight. Also a competent salary for the surgeon and his chest of medicaments, which usually is rated at two hundred or two hundred and fifty pieces of eight. Lastly they stipulate in writing what recompense or reward each one ought to have, that is either wounded or maimed in his body, suffering the loss of any limb, by that voyage. Thus they order for the loss of a right arm six hundred pieces of eight, or six slaves; for the loss of a left arm five hundred pieces of eight, or five slaves; for a right leg five hundred pieces of eight, or five slaves; for a left leg four hundred pieces-of-eight, or four slaves; for an eye one hundred pieces of eight, or one slave; for a finger of the hand the same reward as for the eye. All which sums of money, as I have said before, are taken out of the capital sum or common stock of what is got by their piracy. For a very exact and equal dividend is made of the remainder among them all. Yet herein they have also regard to qualities and places. Thus the Captain, or chief Commander, is allotted five or six portions to what the ordinary seamen have; the Master's Mate only two; and other Officers proportionate to their employment. After whom they draw equal parts from the highest even to the lowest mariner, the boys not being omitted. For even these draw half a share, by reason that, when they happen to take a better vessel than their own, it is the duty of the boys to set fire to the ship or boat wherein they are, and then retire to the prize which they have taken.

They observe among themselves very good orders. For in the prizes they take, it is severely prohibited to every one to usurp anything in particular to themselves. Hence all they take is equally divided, according to what has been said before. Yea, they make a solemn oath to each other not to abscond, or conceal the least thing they find amongst the prey. If afterwards any one is found unfaithful, who has contravened the said oath, immediately he is separated and turned out of the society. Among themselves they are very civil and charitable to each other. Insomuch that if any wants what another has, with great liberality they give it one to another. As soon as these Pirates have taken any prize of ship or boat, the first thing they endeavour is to set on shore the prisoners, detaining only some few for their own help and service, to whom also they give their liberty after the space of two or three years. They put in very frequently for refreshment at one island or another, but more especially into those which lie on the Southern side of the isle of Cuba. Here they careen their vessels, and in the meanwhile some of them go to hunt, others to cruize upon the seas in canoes, seeking their fortune. Many times they take the poor fishermen of tortoises, and, carrying them to their habitations, they make them work so long as the Pirates are pleased.

John Esquemeling [Alexander Exquemelin], *The Buccaneers of America*. London: George Allen & Company, 1911, pp. 58–60.

Doc. 4: *Deposition of Adam Baldridge, Taken May 5, 1699*

In 1690, Adam Baldridge had landed in Madagascar and soon afterward established a post on St. Mary's Island to trade with pirates and slavers coming from the American colonies. Over the next several years he did business with some of the most notorious pirates of the age, including William Kidd, Henry Every, Thomas Tew, Robert Culliford, and George Raynor. By 1699, when he made this deposition, Baldridge had quit Madagascar and had settled down as a respectable citizen of New York. The following selections from his testimony depict the brisk business among traders and pirates on St. Mary's in the last decade of the seventeenth century.

July the 17th 1690. I, Adam Baldridge, arrived at the Island of St. Maries in the ship *fortune*, Richard Conyers Commander, and on the 7th of January 1690/1 I left the ship, being minded to settle among the Negros at St. Maries with two men more, but the ship went to Port Dolphin[1] and was Cast away, April the 15th 1691, and haife the men drownded and haife saved their lives and got a shore, but I continued with the Negros at St. Maries and went to War with them. before my goeing to War one of the men dyed that went a shore with me, and the other being discouraged went on board againe and none continued with me but my Prentice John King.

[1] Fort Dauphin, at the southeast point of Madagascar, had been built by the French.

March the 9th they sailed for Bonnovolo on Madagascar, 16 Leagues from St. Maries, where they stopt to take in Rice. after I went to war six men more left the Ship, whereof two of them dyed about three weeks after they went ashore and the rest dyed since. In May [16]91 I returned from War and brought 70 head of Cattel and some slaves, then I had a house built and settled upon St. Maries, where great store of Negros resorted to me from the Island Madagascar and settled the Island St. Maries, where I lived quietly with them, helping them to redeem their Wives and Children that were taken before my coming to St. Maries by other Negros to the northward of us about 60 Leagues.

October 13, 1691. Arrived the *Batchelors delight,* Captain Georg Raynor[2] Commander, Burden 180 Tons or there abouts, 14 Guns, 70 or 80 men, that had made a voyage into the Red Seas and taken a ship belonging to the Moors, as the men did report, where they took as much money as made the whole share run about 1100 [£]. a man. they Careened at St. Maries, and while they Careened I supplyed them with Cattel for their present spending and they gave me for my Cattel a quantity of Beads, five great Guns for a fortification, some powder and shott, and six Barrells of flower, about 70 barrs of Iron. the ship belonged to Jamaica and set saile from St. Maries November the 4th 1691, bound for Port Dolphin on Madagascar to take in their provision, and December [16]91 they set saile from Port Dolphin bound for America, where I have heard since they arrived at Carolina and Complyed with the owners, giveing them for Ruin of the Ship three thousand pounds, as I have heard since.

* * *

August 7th 1693. Arrived the Ship *Charles,* John Churcher master, from New York, Mr. Fred. Phillips,[3] owner, sent to bring me severall sorts of goods. She had two Cargos in her, one Consigned to said Master to dispose of, and one to me, containing as followeth:

---

[2] George Raynor, who was associated with both Tew and Every, later returned to New York, where Governor Fletcher released his chest of treasure in return for a bribe.

[3] Frederick Philipse (1626–1702) was the richest merchant in New York at the time, but not the least scrupulous. It was said that Baldridge's post in Madagascar was maintained by Philipse's capital so as to obtain a share of the pirates' take.

44 paire of shooes and pumps, 6 Dozen of worsted and threed stockens, 3 dozen of speckled shirts and Breaches, 12 hatts, some Carpenters Tools, 5 Barrells of Rum, four Quarter Caskes of Madera Wine, ten Cases of Spirits, Two old Stills full of hols, one worme, Two Grindstones, Two Cross Sawes and one Whip saw, three Jarrs of oyle, two small Iron Potts, three Barrells of Cannon powder, some books, Catechisms, primers and home books, two Bibles, and some garden Seeds, three Dozen of howes [hoes], and I returned for the said goods 1100 pieces 8/8 and Dollers, 34 Slaves, 15 head of Cattel, 57 barrs of Iron. October the 5th he set sail from St. Maries, after having sold parte of his Cargo to the White men upon Madagascar, to Mauratan to take in Slaves.

October 19, 1693. Arrived the ship *Amity*, Captain Thomas Tew[4] Commander, Burden 70 Tons, 8 Guns, 60 men, haveing taken a Ship in the Red Seas that did belong to the Moors, as the men did report, they took as much money in her as made the whole share run 1200 [£] a man. they Careened at St. Maries and had some cattel from me, but for their victualing and Sea Store they bought from the Negros. I sold Captain Tew and his Company some of the goods brought in the *Charles* from New York. the Sloop belonged most of her to Bermudas. Captain Tew set saile from St. Maries December the 23d 1693, bound for America.

* * *

December 11th 1695. Arrived the Sloop *Amity*, haveing no Captain, her former Captain Thomas Tew being killed by a great Shott from a Moors ship, John Yarland master, Burden seventy Ton, 8 Guns, as before described, and about 60 men. They stayed but five dayes at St. Maries and set saile to seek the *Charming Mary* and they met her at Mauratan on Madagascar and took her, giveing Captain Glover the Sloop to carry him and his men home and all that he had, keeping nothing but the ship. they made a new Commander after they had taken the ship, one Captain Bobbington. after they

---

[4] Tew was a notorious pirate who operated out of Jamaica, Rhode Island, and New York, often with a privateering commission in his hands. Edward Randolph, the Surveyor-General of Customs in the American colonies, reported that from this Red Sea voyage Tew brought £10,000 in gold and silver into Rhode Island. He had sailed with a privateering commission from Governor Fletcher of New York, though the governor undoubtedly had known of Tew's piratical habits.

had taken the ship they went into St. Augustine Bay and there fitted the ship and went into the Indies to make a voyage and I have heard since that they were trapaned and taken by the Moors.[5]

December 29 1695. Arrived a Moors Ship, taken by the *Resolution* and given to Captain Robert Glover[6] and 24 of his men that was not willing to goe a privateering upon the Coasts of Indies, to carrie them away. the Company turned Captain Glover and these 24 men out of the Ship, Captain Glover being parte Owner and Commander of the same and Confined prisoner by his Company upon the Coast of Guinea by reason he would not consent to goe about the Cape of good hope into the Red Sea. the ship was old and would hardly swim with them to St. Maries. when they arrived there they applyed themselves to me. I maintained them in my house with provision till June, that shiping arrived for to carry them home.

J. Franklin Jameson, ed., *Privateering and Piracy in the Colonial Period: Illustrative Documents*. New York: Macmillan Company, 1923, pp. 180–185.

Doc. 5: *John Dann's Testimony against Henry Every*

Henry Every—alias Henry Avery, John Avery, John Every, Long Ben, and Captain Bridgeman—was one of the most colorful of all pirates. Although he is not as well remembered today as Captain Kidd or Blackbeard, during his own lifetime he became rather famous. His life is told in Captain Charles Johnson's History of the Pyrates *(1724), as well as in popular ballads and plays. Believed to have been a native of Devonshire, Every started out as an honest sailor and had already advanced in rank before turning pirate. In 1694, the crew aboard the* Charles *on which he was master mutinied and elected him*

[5] Because the *Amity* had been severely damaged in battle with the "Moors," her crew decided to seize the *Charming Mary*, a well-armed merchant ship from New York. In exchange, the pirates gave Captain Richard Glover (not to be confused with the pirate Robert Glover) the *Amity*. After a successful pirating cruise in the Indian Ocean, the *Charming Mary* sailed to Barbados in 1697, where the booty was divided into shares of roughly £700 per man. The ship was not taken by Moors but was a year later cruising again in the Indian Ocean, now captained by William May.

[6] Robert Glover had been a successful privateersman during King William's War, at which time he gained a reputation for dishonesty. He later turned pirate; but after a disappointing cruise in the Red Sea in 1695, his crew mutinied and chose Dirk Chivers as captain.

FIGURE 8

The Pirate Henry Every (Charles Johnson, *A General History of the Lives and Adventures of the Most Famous Highwaymen, Murderers, Street Robbers, &c.* London: Printed for and sold by O. Payne, 1736. New York Public Library, Rare Books Division.)

captain. They renamed the ship the Fancy *and set course for the Indian Ocean. By 1696, after Every and other pirates had pillaged Mogul ships in the Red Sea, the English East India Company petitioned the home government to suppress the pirates, and in particular Every, as they were detrimental to legitimate trade. A proclamation was issued in July, declaring that Every and his crew were pirates and ordering colonial governors to seize them. Several of the crew were apprehended, tried, and hanged in November. Others found a refuge in the colonies, despite the proclamation. The following selection comes from the testimony of John Dann, who served under Every in the Indian Ocean. Dann points out that the pirates were indiscriminate in whom they attacked. He is also specific in implicating Governor Trott of the Bahamas in aiding the pirates to escape justice. Every did not end up on the gallows like some of his comrades. He was never caught, but vanished from the pages of history into legend, one of the few successful pirates.*

This Informant [John Dann] saith that 3 yeares agoe he was Coxwain in the *Soldado* Prize, That he deserted the said shipp to goe in Sir James Houblons[1] Service, upon an Expedition to the West Indies, under Don Authuro Bourne, hee went on board the *James*, Captain Gibson Commander, and the whole Company shifted their Ship in the Hope, and went on board the *Charles* in which they went to the Corunna [Coruña]. The Shipps Company mutinied at Corunna for want of their pay, there being 8 months due to them; some of the men proposed to Captain Every, who was master [i.e., navigating officer] of the *Charles*, to carry away the Shipp, which was agreed on and sworne too; accordingly they sayled from the Corunna the 7th of May 1693 [1694] when they were gone out they made up about 85 men. Then they asked Captain Gibson, the Commander, whether he was willing to goe with them, which he refusing, they sett him a shoar, with 14 or 15 more.

The first place they came to was the Isle of May [in the Cape Verde Islands], where they mett three English Ships and tooke some provisions out of them, with an Anchor and Cable and about 9 men. They went next to the Coast of Guinea, and there they tooke about 5 li. [litre?] of Gold Dust, under the pretence of Trade;

---

[1] An alderman of London and a director of the Bank of England.

* * * from thence they went to Princes Island,[2] where they mett with 2 Deanes [Danish] ships, which they tooke after some restraine. in those Shipps they tooke some small Armes, Chestes of Lynnen and perpetuenes [a durable woolen fabric], with about 40 l[lbs]. in Gold dust and a great quantity of Brandy, they putt them on shoar Except 18 or 20 they tooke with them.[3] they carryed the best of the Danes Shipps with them and burnt the other. They stood then for Cape Lopez, and in the way mett with a small portugeese [vessel], laden with slaves from Angola, they tooke some Cloathes and silkes from them and gave them some provisions which they were in want of. * * * They went next to Annabo [Annobon] and takeing provisions there they doubled the Cape and sailed to Madagascar, where they tooke more provisions and cleared the ship. from thence they sailed to Johanna, where they mett a small Junke [an Asian trading vessel], put her a shore and tooke 40 peices out of her, and had one of their men killed, they only tooke in provisions at Johanna. Three English Merchant ships came downe thither at the same time, but they did not speake with them. * * * Then they resolved to goe for the Red Sea. in the way they mett with two English Privateers, the one called the *Dolphin*, the other *Portsmouth Adventure*. The *Dolphin*, Captaine Want Comander, was a Spanish Bottom, had 60 men on board and was fitted out at the Orkells[4] neare Philadelphia. She came from thence about 2 yeares agoe last January. The *Portsmouth Adventure* was fitted out at Rhode Island about the same time, Captain Joseph Faro [Farrell] Comander. this ship had about the like number of men and about 6 Gunns each and they joyned Company [with Every]. They came to an Island called Liparan [Perim], at the entrance into the Red Sea, about June last was 12 months, they lay there one night and then 3 sale [sail] more of English came to them, One comanded by Thomas Wake fitted out from Boston in New England, another the *Pearle* Brigantine, William Mues [May] Comander, fitted out of Rhode Island, the third was the *Amity* Sloop, Thomas Tew Comander, fitted out at New Yorke. they

[2] The islands of St. Thome, Principe, and Annobon.

[3] Fourteen Danes joined the pirate crew; according to a letter from the East India Company, dated August 7, 1696, Every's motley gang included 52 French, 14 Danes, the 104 English, Scottish, and Irish seamen.

[4] Whorekill, which is Lewes Creek, Delaware.

had about 6 Guns each. two of them had 50 men on board and the Brigantine betweene 30 and 40. they all Joyned in partnership, agreeing Captain Every should be the Comander. * * * After they had lain there 5 or 6 dayes the Moores shipps (being about 25 in number) past by them in the night unseen, though the passage was not above 2 miles over. they [this] was in August last on Saturday night, the next morning they saw a Ketch comeing downe, which they tooke, and by them they heard the ships were gone by, whereupon it was resolved they should all follow them and accordingly they wheighed on Monday[.] * * * they steered their Course for Suratt, whether the Moores ships were bound, about 3 dayes before they made Cape St. John [Cape Diu?] they mett with one of the Moores ships [i.e., the *Fateh Mohammed*], betweene 2 and 300 tons, with 6 Guns, which they tooke, she haveing fired 3 shott. they tooke about 50 or 60,000 [£]. in that ship in Silver and gold, and kept her with them till they made the land, and comeing to an anchor they espied another ship [i.e., the *Gang-i-Saway* or *Gunsway*]. they made sale up to her. she had about 40 Guns mounted and as they said 800 men. Shee stood a fight of 3 houres and then yeilded, the men runing into the Hold and there they made their Voyage. They tooke out of that ship soe much Gold and Silver in Coyned money and Plate [bullion] as made up each mans share with what they had taken before about 1000 [£] a man, there being 180 that had their Dividents, the Captain haveing a Double share and the Master a share and a halfe.[5] The *Portsmouth* did not come into the Fight and therefore had noe Divident, but the Brigantine had, which was taken away from them againe by reason that the *Charles's* men changing with them Silver for Gold they found the Brigantine men Clippt the Gold, soe they left them only 2000 peices of Eight to buy provisions. They gave a share to the Captain of the *Portsmouth* and brought him away with them. Captain Want went into his ship and sailed into the Gulph of Persia and the Brigantine (he thinkes) went to the Coast of Ethiopia. Captain Wake went to the Island of St. Maries near Madagascar, intending for the Red Sea the next time the Moores ships were expected from thence. Captain Every resolved to goe streight for the Island of Providence [in the

---

[5] See the pirate articles in Doc. 9 on the division of spoils.

Bahamas]. In the way the men mutinied, some being for carrying her to Kian [Cayenne] belonging to the French, neere Brazill, but Captain Every withstood it, there being not above 20 men in the Shipp that Joyned with him. when they came to the Island of Mascareen [Réunion] in the Latitude of 21 they left as many men there as had a mind to stay in that Island, and about March or Aprill last they arrived in the Island of Providence [Bahamas] with 113 men on board, they came first to an Anchor off the Island of Thera [Eleuthera], and by a sloop sent a Letter to Nicholas Trott, Governor of Providence,[6] to propose bringing their ship thither if they might be assured of Protection and Liberty to goe away, which he promised them. They made a collection of 20 peices of 8 a man and the Captain 40, to present the Governor with, besides Elephants Teeth and some other things to the value of about 1000 l. Then they left their Ship which the Governor had and 46 Guns in her. they bought a sloop which cost them 600 l. Captain Every and about 20 more came in her for England and Every tooke the name of Bridgman; about 23 more of the men bought another Sloop and with the Master, Captain Risby, and the rest of the men went for Carolina.

J. Franklin Jameson, ed., *Privateering and Piracy in the Colonial Period: Illustrative Documents.* New York: Macmillan Company, 1923, pp. 165–170.

Doc. 6: *Captain William Kidd's Royal Commission, 1695*

William Kidd, who is erroneously referred to below as Robert Kidd, was one of the most notorious pirates to have lived, yet according to some writers he was not a pirate at all—rather a scapegoat who got caught up in the political battles between Whigs and Tories in England at the end of the seventeenth century. There was, indeed, a thin line separating pirate and privateer, and as Adam Baldridge's testimony (Doc. 4) shows, captains who did not abide with the wishes of their crew often were marooned. It is certain that Kidd exceeded his commission in plundering several vessels in the Indian Ocean, but it is uncertain whether he did so under duress from his crew. Kidd received royal commissions

[6] Governor of the Bahamas from 1693 to 1696, when he was removed because of his dealings with pirates.

FIGURE 9

The Hanging of Capt. Kidd (Charles Ellms, *The Pirates Own Book: Authentic Narratives of the Most Celebrated Sea Robbers*. Salem: Maritime Research Society, 1924.)

as a privateer to attack French vessels and, as the document below indicates, to forcefully seize pirates operating at the time in the Red Sea.

William Rex,

William the Third, by the grace of God, King of England, Scotland, France and Ireland, defender of the faith, &c. To our trusty and well beloved Capt. Robert [i.e., William] Kidd, commander of the ship the Adventure galley, or to any other, the commander of the same for the time being, Greeting: Whereas we are informed, that Capt. Thomas Too [Tew], John Ireland, Capt. Thomas Wake, and Capt. William Maze or Mace [or May],[1] and other subjects, natives or inhabitants of New York, and elsewhere, in our plantations in America, have associated themselves with divers others, wicked and ill-disposed persons, and do, against the law of nations, commit many and great piracies, robberies and depredations on the seas upon the parts of America, and in other parts, to the great hindrance and discouragement of trade and navigation, and to the great danger and hurt of our loving subjects, our allies, and all others, navigating the seas upon their lawful occasions. Now Know Ye, that we being desirous to prevent the aforesaid mischiefs, and as much as in us lies, to bring the said pirates, free-booters and sea-rovers to justice, have thought fit, and do hereby give and grant to the said Robert Kidd, (to whom our commissioners for exercising the office of Lord High Admiral of England, have granted a commission as a private man-of-war, bearing date the 11th day of December, 1695,) and unto the commander of the said ship for the time being, and unto the officers, mariners, and others which shall be under your command, full power and authority to apprehend, seize, and take into your custody as well the said Capt. Thomas Too, John Ireland, Capt. Thomas Wake, and Capt. Wm. Maze or Mace, as all such pirates, free-booters, and sea-rovers, being either our subjects, or of other nations associated with them, which you shall meet with upon the seas or coasts of America, or upon any other seas or coasts, with all their ships and vessels, and all such

---

[1] In 1695, these men were all wanted pirates who had consorted with Henry Every for attacks on Mogul ships in the Indian Ocean. They had all set sail from the American colonies earlier that same year, in some cases with privateering commissions that had been issued by governors of New York, Rhode Island, and elsewhere.

merchandizes, money, goods, and wares as shall be found on board, or with them, in case they shall willingly yield themselves; but if they will not yield without fighting, then you are by force to compel them to yield. And we also require you to bring, or cause to be brought, such pirates, free-booters, or sea-rovers, as you shall seize, to a legal trial, to the end they may be proceeded against according to the law in such cases. And we do hereby command all our officers, ministers, and other our loving subjects whatsoever, to be aiding and assisting to you in the premises. And we do hereby enjoin you to keep an exact journal of your proceedings in execution of the premises, and set down the names of such pirates, and of their officers and company, and the names of such ships and vessels as you shall by virtue of these presents take and seize, and the quantities of arms, ammunition, provision, and lading of such ships, and the true value of the same, as near as you judge. And we do hereby strictly charge and command you, as you will answer the contrary at your peril, that you do not, in any manner, offend or molest our friends or allies, their ships or subjects, by colour or pretence of these presents, or the authority thereby granted. In witness whereof, we have caused our great seal of England to be affixed to these presents. Given at our court in Kensington, the 26th day of January, 1695, in the 7th year of our reign.[2]

[Charles Ellms,] *The Pirates Own Book, or, Authentic Narratives of the Lives, Exploits, and Executions of the Most Celebrated Sea Robbers*. Salem: Maritime Research Society, 1924, pp. 172–174.

Doc. 7: *Captain William Snelgrave's Captivity, 1719*

On April 1, 1719, during that last great surge in Western piracy, William Snelgrave's vessel, the Bird Galley, *was seized by pirates at the mouth of the Sierra Leone River in West Africa. While some of his crew joined with the pirates, Snelgrave and most of his men were made prisoners and detained for a*

[2] Besides this royal commission for the seizure of pirates anywhere in the world, Kidd received two other commissions: one issued by the Admiralty allowing him to plunder French vessels while at war, and the other a royal commission granting Kidd's partners, Lord Bellomont and others, the right to keep all ships and booty seized by Kidd. This last document was extraordinary because it allowed the partners to take ownership of the prizes without going through normal legal procedures or paying the requisite fees to the Admiralty.

month. During his captivity Snelgrave was able to closely observe the workings and habits of his captors, an account of which he published in 1734. His book remains one of the best firsthand sources on pirates ever written. He candidly depicts their rugged democracy and egalitarianism in action, as well as their fits of cruelty and nearly constant debauchery.

About five a Clock in the Afternoon [April 1, 1719], a small Breeze arising from the Sea, and the Tide of Flood setting strong, we stood for the [Sierra Leone] River's Mouth. At Sun-setting we perceived a Ship at Anchor, a great way up the River; which was the Pirate that took us soon after. The other two Pirate Ships, with their Prizes, were hid from our sight by a Point of Land.[1]

* * *

[That night] the Pirates immediately boarded us, and coming on the Quarter-deck, fired their Pieces several times down into the Steerage, and shot a Sailor in the Reins, of which Wound he died afterwards. They likewise threw several Granado-shells, which burst amongst us, so that 'tis a great wonder several of us were not killed by them, or by their Shot.

At last some of our People bethought themselves to call out for *Quarter*, which the Pirates granting, the *Quarter-master* came down into the Steerage, enquiring, "Where the Captain was?" I told him, "I had been so till now." Upon that he asked me, "How I durst order my People to fire at their Boat out of the Steerage? saying, that they had heard me repeat it several times." I answered, "I thought it my Duty to defend the Ship, if my People would have fought." Upon that he presented a Pistol to my Breast, which I had but just time to parry before it went off; so that the Bullet past between my Side and Arm. The Rogue finding he had not shot me, he turned the But-end of the Pistol, and gave me such a Blow on the Head as stunned me; to that I fell upon my Knees; but immediately recovering my self, I forthwith jumped out of the Steerage upon the Quarter-deck, where the Pirate Boatswain was.

He was a bloody Villain, having a few days before killed a poor Sailor, because he did not do something so soon as he had ordered

---

[1] The three pirate ships were those commanded by Thomas Cocklyn, Oliver La Buse, and Howell Davis. Snelgrave's ship was seized by Cocklyn's crew.

him. This cruel Monster was asking some of my People, "Where their Captain was." So at my coming upon Deck, one of them, pointing to me, said, "There he is." Tho' the night was very dark, yet there being four Lanthorns with Candles, he had a full sight of me: Whereupon lifting up his broad Sword, he swore, "No Quarter should be given to any Captain that offered to defend his Ship," aiming at the same time a full stroke at my Head. To avoid it I stooped so low, that the Quarter-deck Rail received the Blow; and was cut in at least an inch deep: Which happily saved my Head from being cleft asunder: And the Sword breaking at the same time, with the force of the Blow on the Rail, it prevented his cutting me to pieces.

By good Fortune his Pistols, that hung at his Girdle, were all discharged; otherwise he would doubtless have shot me. But he took one of them, and with the But-end endeavoured to beat out my Brains, which some of my People that were then on the Quarter-deck observing, cried out aloud, "For God's sake don't kill our Captain, for we never were with a better Man." This turned the Rage of him and two other Pirates on my People, and saved my Life: But they cruelly used my poor Men, cutting and beating them unmercifully.

* * *

Then the Quarter-master took me by the hand, and told me, "My Life was safe provided none of my People complained against me." I replied, "I was sure none of them could."

The Pirates next, loaded all their small Arms, and fired several Vollies for Joy they had taken us.

* * *

As soon as the Pirate-ship had done firing, I asked the Quarter-master's leave[.] * * * Just after that, a person came to me from the Quarter-master, desiring to know, "What a Clock it was by my Watch?" Which judging to be a civil way of demanding it, I sent it him immediately: desiring the Messenger to tell him, it was a very good going Gold Watch. When it was delivered to the Quarter-master, he held it up by the Chain, and presently laid it down on the Deck, giving it a kick with his Foot; saying, "It was a pretty Football: On which, one of the Pirates caught it up, saying," He would put it in the common Chest to be sold at the Mast.

* * *

By this time I was loudly called upon to go on board the Pirate-ship. * * * Then I was ordered to go on the Quarter-deck to their Commander [Thomas Cocklyn], who saluted me in this manner. "I am sorry you have met with bad usage after Quarter given, but 'tis the Fortune of War sometimes. I expect you will answer truly to all such Questions as I shall ask you: otherwise you shall be cut to pieces, but if you tell the Truth, and your Men make no Complaints against you, you shall be kindly used; and this shall be the best Voyage you ever made in your Life, as you shall find by what shall be given you." I thanked him for his good Intentions, telling him, "I was content to stand on the footing he had proposed to me."

* * *

As soon as I had done answering the Captain's Questions, a tall Man, with four Pistols in his Girdle, and a broad Sword in his Hand, came to me on the Quarter-deck, telling me, "His name was *James Griffin*, and that we had been Schoolfellows." * * * [T]he Captain desired Mr. *Griffin* my Schoolfellow to show me the way to the great Cabbin, and he followed himself.

There was not in the Cabbin either Chair, or any thing else to sit upon, for they always kept a clear Ship ready for an Engagement: So a Carpet was spread on the Deck, upon which we sat down cross-legg'd. Captain *Cocklyn* drank my Health, desiring, "I would not be cast down at my Misfortune, for one of the Boat's Crew who had taken us had told him, My Ship's Company in general spoke well of me, and they had Goods enough left in the Ships they had taken to make a Man of me." Then he drank several other Healths, amongst which was that of the *Pretender*, by the name of King *James the Third*, and thereby I found they were doubly on the side of the Gallows, both as Traitors and Pirates.[2]

---

[2] As this toast indicates, there was a strong streak of Jacobitism among some English pirates of this period. Jacobites wanted to overthrow the settlement that had brought the Hanoverian George I as the king of England in 1714; they led two uprisings that coincided with this phase of piracy.

It being by this time Midnight, my Schoolfellow desired the Captain, "To have a Hammock hung up for me to sleep in;" for it seems every one lay rough, as they called it, that is, on the Deck; the Captain himself not being allowed a Bed. This being granted, and soon after done, I took leave of the Captain, and got into the Hammock, tho' I could not sleep in my melancholy Circumstances. Moreover, the execrable Oaths and Blasphemies I heard among the Ship's Company, shock'd me to such a decree, that in Hell it felt I thought there could not be worse, for tho' many Seafaring Men are given to swearing and taking God's Name in vain, yet I could not have imagined, human Nature could ever so far degenerate, as to talk in the manner those abandoned Wretches did.

* * *

As soon as the Fumes of the Liquor were gone out of the Pirates Heads, they all went on board the Prize, as they called my Ship, about eight a clock in the morning, it being the second day of *April*. Mr. *Jones*, who had been my first Mate, went with them [i.e., had joined the pirates]; and he having confirmed them in their intention of keeping the Ship for their own use, all hands went to work to clear the Ship, by throwing overboard Bales of Woollen Goods, Cases of *India* Goods; with many other things of great Value: So that before night they had destroyed between three and four thousand Pounds worth of the Cargoe. For they had little regard to these things, Money and Necessaries being what they chiefly wanted.

* * *

Soon after this, *Captain Cocklyn* with his Quarter-master and others, came from the Prize on board their old Ship, to compliment Captain *Davis* and the rest that came with him. After the Compliments were over, Captain *Davis* generously said, "He was ashamed to hear how I had been used by them. That they should remember, their Reasons for going a pirating were to revenge themselves on base Merchants, and cruel Commanders of Ships."

* * *

[The next day] I was awaked early in the Morning by a great number of Captain *Davis*'s Crew, who came on board to take part

of the Liquors and Necessaries, according to Agreement. It was
very surprizing to see the Actions of these People. They and *Cocklyn*'s Crew (for *Le Boofe*'s were not yet admitted) made such Waste
and Destruction, that I am sure a numerous set of such Villains
would in a short time, have ruined a great City. They hoisted upon
Deck a great many half Hogsheads of *Claret*, and *French Brandy*;
knock'd their Heads out, and dipp'd Canns and Bowls into them to
drink out of: And in their Wantonness threw full Buckets of each
sort upon one another. As soon as they had emptied what was on
the Deck, they hoisted up more: And in the evening washed the
Decks with what remained in the Casks. As to bottled Liquor of
many sorts, they made such havock of it, that in a few days they had
not one Bottle left: For they would not give themselves the trouble
of drawing the Cork out, but nick'd the Bottles, as they called it,
that is, struck their necks off with a Cutlace; by which means one
in three was generally broke: Neither was there any Cask-liquor left
in a short time, but a little *French* Brandy.

As to Eatables, such as Cheese, Butter, Sugar, and many other
things, they were as soon gone. For the Pirates being all in a
drunken Fit, which held as long as the Liquor lasted, no care was
taken by any one to prevent this Destruction: Which they repented
of when too late.

* * *

Amongst my Adventure of Goods, I had in a Box three second-
hand embroidered Coats. One day the three Pirate Captains, coming on board the Prize together, enquired for them, saying, "They
understood by my Book such Clothes were in my Ship." I told
them, "They were in a Box under the bed place in the State-room.
So they ordered them to be taken out, and immediately put them
on." But the longest Coat falling to *Cocklyn*'s share, who was a very
short Man, it almost reached as low as his Ancles. This very much
displeased him, and he would fain have changed with *Le Boofe*,
or *Davis*: But they refused, telling him, "As they were going on
Shore amongst the *Negroe-Ladies*, who did not know the white Mens
fashions, it was no matter. Moreover, as his Coat was Scarlet
embroidered with Silver, they believed he would have the prefer-
ence of them, (whose Coats were not so showy) in the opinion of

their Mistresses." This making him easy, they all went on Shore together.

It is a Rule amongst the Pirates, not to allow Women to be on board their Ships, when in the Harbour. And if they should take a Prize at Sea, that has any Women on board, no one dares, on pain of death, to force them against their Inclinations.[3] This being a good political Rule to prevent disturbances amongst them, it is strictly observed. So now being in a Harbour, they went on Shore to the Negroe-women, who were very fond of their Company, for the sake of the great Presents they gave them. Nay, some white Men that lived there, did not scruple to lend their black Wives to the Pirates, purely on account of the great Rewards they gave.

The Pirate Captains having taken these Cloaths without leave from the Quarter-master, it gave great Offence to all the Crew; who alledg'd, "If they suffered such things, the Captains would for the future assume a Power, to take whatever they liked for themselves." So, upon their returning on board next Morning, the Coats were taken from them, and put into the common Chest, to be sold at the Mast.

* * *

The 29th of *April*, such of the Pirates as were my Friends, sent me word on Shore, "That the Sale of Necessaries was to begin that day in the afternoon, in the *Windham-Galley* [as the pirates had renamed Snelgrave's ship], Captain *Cocklyn*." So I went on board in a large Cannoe, belonging to two Men that lived ashore, who went at the same time with me. At the Sale, several of the Pirates bought many Necessaries that had been mine, and gave them to me. Likewise, Mr. *James Griffin*, my Schoolfellow, was so civil as to beg from those that were not so kind to me, as he hoped they would have been. The two white Men that went with me in the Cannoe, minded their own business so well, that they got several great Bundles of Clothes and Goods, which they put into the Cannoe with mine.

By this time several Pirates being half drunk with Brandy, looked over the side, and seeing so many Bundles in the Cannoe, which

---

[3] Apparently such regulations were common among the pirates, as were the harsh punishments for transgressors; see Doc. 9.

they supposed to be all mine, they swore, "I was insatiable, and that it would be a good deed to throw them overboard." This my kind Schoolfellow hearing, he came and told me of it, advising me, to go immediately on Shore, which I accordingly did, and it proved very happy for me. For soon after my Watch was put up to sale, and many bidding for it, some of them out of Spite to Captain *Davis*, it was run up to one hundred Pounds, which he paid down.

* * *

The next morning early, which was the last day of *April*, * * * I was agreeably surprized with the arrival of one Mr. *James Bleau*, my Surgeon.

* * *

Mr. Bleau brought us the agreeable News, that the three Pirate Ships, with their Tender, were under sail, going out of the River. This gave us all on Shore the highest Satisfaction; for I had been then in their hands a Month, and many others much longer.

William Snelgrave, *A New Account of Some Parts of Guinea, and the Slave-Trade*. London: Printed for James, John, and Paul Knapton, at the Crown in Ludgate Street, 1734, pp. 201–280. Huntington Library, Rare Books Collection.

Doc. 8: *The Life of Mary Read*

Mary Read and Anne Bonny, the two most famous female pirates during the age of sail, had dressed as boys since youth and as such later on went to sea seeking freedom and fortune. Although the story of Mary Read's life, which is taken from Charles Johnson's History *of the* Pyrates, *may not be reliable in all its details, it was nonetheless based largely on actual trial records and stories that circulated on docksides. The stories of Read and Bonny have fascinated generations of readers and scholars, just as they have served everyone from Whig historians seeking justifications against the evils of piracy to feminists seeking historical role models. (See Jo Stanley's essay in Part 3.) The selection below recounts Mary Read's life as a soldier, sailor, privateersman, and pirate.*

Mary Read was born in *England*, her Mother was married young, to a Man who used the Sea, who going a Voyage soon after their Marriage, left her with Child, which Child prov'd to be a Boy. As to the Husband, whether he was cast away, or died in the Voyage, *Mary Read* could not tell; but however, he never returned more; nevertheless, the Mother, who was young and airy, met with an Accident, which has often happen'd to Women who are young, and do not take a great deal of Care; which was, she soon proved with Child again, without a Husband to Father it, but how, or by whom, none but her self could tell, for she carried a pretty good Reputation among her Neighbours. Finding her Burthen grew, in order to conceal her Shame, she takes a formal Leave of her Husbands Relations, giving out, that she went to live with some Friends of her own, in the Country: Accordingly she went away, and carried with her her young Son, at this Time, not a Year old: Soon after her Departure her Son died, but Providence in Return, was pleased to give her a Girl in his Room, of which she was safely delivered, in her Retreat, and this was our *Mary Read*.

Here the Mother liv'd three or four Years, till what Money she had was almost gone; then she thought of returning to *London*, and considering that her Husband's Mother was in some Circumstances, she did not doubt but to prevail upon her, to provide for the Child, if she could but pass it upon her for the same, but the changing a Girl into a Boy, seem'd a difficult Piece of Work, and how to deceive an experienced old Woman, in such a Point, was altogether as impossible; however, she ventured to dress it up as a Boy, brought it to Town, and presented it to her Mother in Law, as her Husband's Son; the old Woman would have taken it, to have bred it up, but the Mother pretended it would break her Heart, to part with it; so it was agreed betwixt them, that the Child should live with the Mother, and the supposed Grandmother should allow a Crown a Week for its Maintainance.

Thus the Mother gain'd her Point, she bred up her Daughter as a Boy, and when she grew up to some Sense, she thought proper to let her into the Secret of her Birth, to induce her to conceal her Sex. It happen'd that the Grandmother died, by which Means the Subsistance that came from that Quarter, ceas'd, and they were more and more reduced in their Circumstances; wherefore she was obliged to put her Daughter out, to wait on a *French* Lady, as a Foot-boy, being now thirteen Years of Age: Here she did not live long, for growing bold and strong, and having also a roving Mind, she entered herself on Board a Man of War, where she served some Time, then quitted it, went over to *Flanders*, and carried Arms in a Regiment of Foot, as a *Cadet*, and tho' upon all Actions, she behaved herself with a great deal of Bravery, yet she could not get a Commission, they being generally bought and sold; therefore she quitted the Service, and took on in a Regiment of Horse; she behaved so well, in several Engagements, that she got the Esteem of all her Officers; but her Comrade, who was a *Fleming*, happening to be a handsome young Fellow, she falls in Love with him[.] * * * Love is ingenious, and as they lay together in the same Tent, and were constantly together, she found a Way of letting him discover her Sex, without appearing that it was done with Design.

* * *

[Soon afterwards they married, and] easily obtain'd their Discharge, and they immediately set up an Eating House or Ordinary, which was the Sign of the *Three Horse-Shoes*, near the Castle in *Breda*, where they soon run into a good Trade, a great many Officers eating with them constantly.

But this Happiness lasted not long, for the Husband soon died, and the Peace of *Reswick*[1] being concluded, there was no Resort of Officers to *Breda*, as usual, so that the Widow having little or no Trade, was forced to give up House-keeping, and her Substance being by Degrees quite spent, she again assumes her Man's Apparel, and * * * [after serving briefly in the Dutch army] ships herself on board of a Vessel bound for the *West-Indies*.

It happen'd this Ship was taken by *English* Pyrates, and *Mary Read* being the only *English* Person on Board, they kept her amongst them, and having plundered the Ship, let it go again; after following this Trade for some Time, the King's Proclamation [probably 1717] came out, and was publish'd in all Parts of the *West-Indies*, for pardoning such Pyrates, who should voluntarily surrender themselves by a certain Day therein mentioned. The Crew of *Mary Read*,

[1] Treaty of Ryswick (1697) ended one of the many European wars at the time involving England, France, Holland, and Spain.

took the Benefit of this Proclamation, and having surrender'd, liv'd quietly on Shore; but Money beginning to grow short, and hearing that Captain *Woodes Rogers*, Governor of the Island of *Providence*, was fitting out some Privateers, to cruise against the *Spaniards*, she, with several others, embark'd for that Island, in order to go upon the privateering Account, being resolved to make her Fortune one way or other.

These Privateers were no sooner sail'd out, but the Crews of some of them, who had been pardoned, rose against their Commanders, and turned themselves to their old Trade: In this Number was *Mary Read*. It is true, she often declared, that the Life of a Pyrate was what she always abhor'd, and went into it only upon Compulsion, both this Time, and before, intending to quit it, whenever a fair Opportunity should offer it self; yet some of the Evidence against her, upon her Tryal, who were forced Men, and had sail'd with her, deposed upon Oath, that in Times of Action, no Person amongst them was more resolute, or ready to board or undertake any Thing that was hazardous, than she and *Anne Bonny*; and particularly at the time they were attack'd and taken, when they came to close Quarters, none kept the Deck except *Mary Read*, and *Anne Bonny*, and one more; upon which, she, *Mary Read*, called to those under Deck, to come up and fight like Men, and finding they did not stir, fired her Arms down the Hold amongst them, killing one, and wounding others.

This was Part of the Evidence against her, which she denied; which, whether true or no, thus much is certain, that she did not want Bravery, nor indeed was she less remarkable for her Modesty, according to the Notions of Virtue: Her Sex was not so much as suspected by any Person on board till *Anne Bonny*, who was not altogether so reserv'd in Point of Chastity, took a particular Liking to her; in short, *Anne Bonny* took her for a handsome young Fellow, and for some Reasons best known to herself, first discovered her Sex to *Mary Read*; *Mary Read* knowing what she would be at, * * * she let her know she was a Woman also; but this Intimacy so disturb'd Captain *Rackam*, who was the Lover and Gallant of *Anne Bonny*, that he grew furiously jealous, so that he told *Anne Bonny*, he would cut her new Lover's Throat, therefore, to quiet him, she let him into the Secret also.

Captain *Rackam*, (as he was enjoined,) kept the Thing a Secret from all the Ships Company, yet, notwithstanding all her Cunning and Reserve, Love found her out in this Disguise, and hinder'd her from forgetting her Sex. In their Cruize they took a great Number of Ships, belonging to *Jamaica*, and other Parts of the *West-Indies*, bound to, and from *England*; and when ever they met any good Artist [artisan], or other Person that might be of any great Use to their Company, if he was not willing to enter, it was their Custom to keep him by Force. Among these was a young Fellow, of a most engaging Behaviour, or, at least, he was so in the Eyes of *Mary Read*, who became so smitten with his Person and Address, that she could neither rest Night or Day; [and so decided] * * * to find a Way to let him discover her Sex: She first insinuated herself into his Liking, by talking against the Life of a Pyrate, which he was altogether averse to, so they became Mess-Mates, and strict Companions: When she found he had a Friendship for her, as a Man, she suffered the Discovery to be made, by carelessly shewing her Breasts, which were very White.

The young Fellow, who was made of Flesh and Blood, had his Curiosity and Desire so rais'd by this Sight, that he never ceas'd importuning her, till she confess'd what she was. Now begins the Scene of Love[.] * * * It happened this young Fellow had a Quarrel with one of the Pyrates, and their Ship then lying at an Anchor, near one of the Islands, they had appointed to go ashore and fight, according to the Custom of the Pyrates:[2] *Mary Read*, was to the last Degree uneasy and anxious, for the Fate of her Lover; she would not have had him refuse the Challenge, because, she could not bear the Thoughts of his being branded with Cowardice; on the other Side, she dreaded the Event, and apprehended the Fellow might be too hard for him: * * * in this Dilemma, she shew'd, that she fear'd more for his Life than she did for her own; for she took a Resolution of quarrelling with this Fellow her self, and having challenged him ashore, she appointed the Time two Hours sooner than that when he was to meet her Lover, where she fought him at Sword and Pistol, and killed him upon the Spot.

---

[2] See, for example, the pirate articles signed by Roberts' gang in Doc. 9.

FIGURE 10

Mary Read Kills Her Lover's Foe (Charles Ellms, *The Pirates Own Book: Authentic Narratives of the Most Celebrated Sea Robbers*. Salem: Maritime Research Society, 1924.)

* * *

If he had no regard for her before, this Action would have bound him to her for ever; but there was no Occasion for Ties or Obligation, his Inclination towards her was sufficient; in fine, they plighted their Troth to each other, which *Mary Read* said, she look'd upon to be as good a Marriage, in Conscience, as if it had been done by a Minister in Church; and to this was owing her great Belly, which she pleaded to save her Life.

* * *

It is no doubt, but many had Compassion for her, yet the Court could not avoid finding her Guilty; for among other Things, one of the Evidences against her, deposed, that being taken by *Rackam*, and detain'd some Time on Board, he fell accidentally into Discourse with *Mary Read*, whom he taking for a young Man, ask'd her, what Pleasure she could have in being concerned in such Enterprizes, where her Life was continually in Danger, by Fire or Sword; and not only so, but she must be sure of dying an ignominious Death, if she should be taken alive?—She answer'd, that as to hanging, she thought it no great Hardship, for, were it not for that, every cowardly Fellow would turn Pyrate, and so infest the Seas, that Men of Courage must starve:—That if it was put to the Choice of the Pyrates, they would not have the Punishment less than Death, the Fear of which, kept some dastardly Rogues honest; that many of those who are now cheating the Widows and Orphans, and oppressing their poor Neighbours, who have no Money to obtain Justice, would then rob at Sea, and the Ocean would be crowded with Rogues, like the Land, and no Merchant would venture out; so that the Trade, in a little Time, would not be worth following.

Being found quick with Child, as has been observed, her Execution was respited, and it is possible she would have found Favour, but she was seiz'd with a violent Feaver, soon after her Tryal, of which she died in Prison.

Charles Johnson, *A General History of the Robberies and Murders of the Most Notorious Pirates, and also their Policies, discipline and Government, from their First Rise and Settlement in the Island of Providence, in 1717, to the Present Year 1724.* London: For C. Rivington, J. Lacy, 1724, pp. 118–126. New York Public Library, Rare Books Division.

Doc. 9: Pirate Articles

Early eighteenth-century pirate articles, such as the ones given below, present strong evidence that at least some pirates acted democratically in an undemocratic age and that there could truly be honor among thieves. Derived perhaps from ancient seafaring traditions, all crew members aboard pirate vessels swore oaths or signed articles at the outset of cruises whereby they agreed on the manner of such matters as discipline and the sharing out of booty. Bartholomew Roberts' articles perhaps went further than most, banning gambling and sex (with either boys or women) on board ship and limiting drinking after eight o'clock at night. The second document comes from John Phillips' gang. On the night of August 29, 1723, Phillips and four companions seized a schooner off Newfoundland that was owned by William Minott of Boston. Once safely out at sea the crew quickly renamed their ship the Revenge, *chose officers, and drew up articles. Phillips was chosen captain and the entire crew then swore to the articles upon a hatchet because they lacked a Bible. Similar to the buccaneers, these early eighteenth-century pirates also included provisions in their articles for pirates who were wounded in battle.*

---

1. Articles aboard Capt. Bartholomew Roberts' *Royal Fortune*, 1720:

[1] *Every Man has a Vote in Affairs of Moment; has equal title to the fresh Provisions, or strong Liquors, at any Time seized, and use of them at Pleasure, unless a Scarcity * * * make it necessary, for the good of all, to Vote a Retrenchment.*

[2] *Every Man to be called fairly in turn, by Lift, on Board of Prizes, because,* (over and above their proper share) *they were on these Occasions allowed a Shift of Cloaths: But if they defrauded the Company to the Value of a Dollar, in Plate, Jewels, or Money, MAROONING was their Punishment. * * * If the Robbery was only between one another, they contented themselves with slitting the Ears or Nose of him that was Guilty, and set him on shore, not in an uninhabited Place, but somewhere, where he was sure to encounter Hardships.*

[3] *No Person to Game at Cards or Dice, for Money.*

[4] *The Lights and Candles to be put out at eight o'Clock at Night: If any of the Crew, after that Hour, still remained inclin'd for Drinking, they were to do it on the open Deck*[.] * * *

[5] *To keep their Piece, Pistols, and Cutlass clean, and fit for Service*[.] * * *

[6] *No Boy or Woman to be allowed amongst them. If any Man were found seducing any of the latter Sex, and carried her to Sea, disguised, he was to suffer Death*[.] * * *

[7] *To Desert the Ship, or their Quarters in Battle, was punished with Death, or Marooning.*

[8] *No striking one another on Board, but every Man's Quarrels to be ended on Shore, at Sword and Pistol*[.] * * *

[9] *No Man to talk of breaking up their Way of Living, till each had shared a 1000 l [£]. If in order to this, any Man should lose a Limb, or become a Cripple in their Service, he was to have 800 Dollars, out of the publick Stock, and for lesser Hurts, proportionably.*

[10] *The Captain and Quarter-Master to receive two Shares of a Prize; the Master, Boatswain, and Gunner, one Share and a half, and other Officers, one and a Quarter.*[1]

---

[1] In a later edition of *The History of the Pyrates*, dated 1742, an eleventh article was included: "The Musicians to have Rest on the Sabbath Day, but the other Six Days and Nights, none, without special Favour."

FIGURE 11
Pirate with a Peg-Leg (Charles Ellms, *The Pirates Own Book: Authentic Narratives of the Most Celebrated Sea Robbers.* Salem: Maritime Research Society, 1924.)

2. Articles aboard Capt. John Phillips' *Revenge*, 1723:

1. Every Man shall obey civil Command; the Captain shall have one full Share and a half in all Prizes; the Master, Carpenter, Boatswain and Gunner shall have one Share and quarter.

2. If any Man shall offer to run away, or keep any Secret from the Company, he shall be maroon'd, with one Bottle of Powder, one Bottle of Water, one small Arm and Shot.

3. If any Man shall steal any Thing in the Company, or game to the Value of a Piece of Eight, he shall be maroon'd or shot.

4. If at any Time we should meet another Marrooner [that is, pyrate], that Man that shall sign his Articles without the Consent of our Company, shall suffer such Punishment as the Captain and Company shall think fit.

5. That Man that shall strike another whilst these Articles are in force, shall receive Moses's Law (that is, 40 Stripes lacking one) on the bare Back.

6. That Man that shall snap his Arms, or smoak Tobacco in the Hold, without a Cap to his Pipe, or carry a Candle lighted without a Lanthorn, shall suffer the same Punishment as in the former Article.

7. That Man that shall not keep his Arms clean, fit for an Engagement, or neglect his Business, shall be cut off from his Share, and suffer such other Punishment as the Captain and the Company shall think fit.

8. If any Man shall lose a Joint in Time of an Engagement, he shall have 400 Pieces of Eight, if a Limb, 800.

9. If at any Time we meet with a prudent Woman, that Man that offers to meddle with her, without her Consent, shall suffer present Death.

Charles Johnson, *A General History of the Robberies and Murders of the Most Notorious Pirates, and also their Policies, discipline and Government, from their First Rise and Settlement in the Island of Providence, in 1717, to the Present Year 1724.* London: For C. Rivington, J. Lacy, 1724, pp. 169–172. New York Public Library, Rare Books Division; and George Francis Dow and John Henry Edmonds, *The Pirates of the New England Coast, 1630–1730.* Salem: Marine Research Society, 1923, pp. 315–316.

Corsairs of the Mediterranean

Doc. 10: *Maltese Corsairing License Issued to Knight Charles de Willers, 1696*

Both Barbary and Christian corsairs were sanctioned by their respective governments for raids against enemy shipping and settlements. Among the Maltese corsairs commissions were issued to both private citizens and knights, allowing them to retain only one-fourth of the value of the prizes captured, the remainder being turned over to the government of Malta. The following excerpt is an English translation of the license granted by Grand Master Raymond de Perellos y Roccafull to the Knight Charles de Willers on February 27, 1696.

Whereas the Knight Charles de Willers was empowered by the Most Eminent Grand Master, our predecessor, to wage war against the Infidel with an armed ship flying the banner of Our Sacred Religion; and whereas his licence to go corsairing was extended for a period of five years; and whereas, finally, the same Knight-Captain was permitted to equip two oar-driven vessels under the Order's flag for the continuation of the war against the Infidel during the above mentioned period, after having taken the customary oath and undertaken, as usual, not to molest the Christians and after having declared his willingness to abide by the obligations contained in the Ordinances, and Decrees of Armaments, We, therefore, in virtue of these presents do confirm and ratify the above-named authority to wage war against the Infidel with his ship and with his two oar-driven vessels during the above-stated period. We also ordain that his ships together with their crews and prizes, be accorded free passage by sea and by land wherever they happen to travel.

Paul Cassar, "The Maltese Corsairs and the Order of St. John of Jerusalem," *The Catholic Historical Review*, July 1960, pp. 150–151.

Doc. 11: *An Episode at Estampalia*

Although the prime targets of the Barbary corsairs were Christian vessels and settlements, and likewise the prime victims of Christian corsairs were Muslim vessels and settlements, this was not always the case. The following episode, from the early seventeenth century, involved a gang of Christian corsairs that raided a Greek town and kidnapped the local priest—an unauthorized act not only because it was against a Christian community but also because the perpetrators acted without a legitimate commission. Alonso de Contreras, a Maltese corsair who hailed from Spain, described this incident in which he intervened on behalf of the Greek Christians.

Arrived at Estampalia [Stampalia, an island near Rhodes with a large settlement of Greeks], I entered the harbour. It was a feast-day; and so soon as they knew that it was I, they took counsel together, and at once there came out almost all the people, with Captain George (for that was the governor's name), calling upon me as *O morfo pulicarto*, which means, 'Young gallant.' * * * They all came sad and weeping, and begging me with much clamour to be their judge; for a frigate of the Christians had carried off by guile their *papaz*—that is, their priest—and had asked for him two thousand sequins.[1] I asked where he was, and when he had been captured. They said, that very morning, and they had not heard mass, and the hour was then two in the afternoon. Again I questioned them, 'Where, then, is the frigate of the Christians which took him away?' They said, 'At the Careenage,' which is an island about two miles away. I turned my frigate thitherwards; and this was quite in order, for I was bound to fight them, Christians though they might be: since they are men who take up arms without a licence, evil-livers all; and they rob both Moors and Christians, as has been seen, since they captured the priest and held him to ransom for two thousand sequins. To cut a long story short, I arrived at the islet with arms in hand and artillery in readiness. I found the frigate flying a flag with the image of Our Lady. She was a little frigate, with nine benches, and a crew of twenty. I at once ordered her captain on board my frigate. He obeyed on the spot, and I asked him where he had fitted his ship. He said, 'At Messina.' I asked him for his commission, and he gave it me; but it was a forged one. Upon this I made half the crew come on board my frigate, and had them put in irons, and I sent a like number on to his frigate. They began to protest, saying that it was not their fault; that Jacomo Panaro—for such was their captain's name—had deceived them Saying that he had a commission from the Viceroy; and that they would go to the end of the world to serve me, but they would not go an inch for the other; that they had not known he intended to capture the priest; and as soon as they had seen my frigate enter the harbour, the captain had wanted to flee with the priest; but they would not do so, and had waited. For these reasons I decided that I would not put them in irons; but I set the captain on shore on the island, naked and with no provisions, so that he should pay for his sin there by dying of hunger. I went off with the two frigates; and when I arrived at the harbour, nearly all the people were gathered together there. I set the priest ashore, and as soon as they saw him they

---

[1] Sequins here refer to gold coins in circulation in Italy and Turkey at the time.

began to cry aloud and bless me a thousand times. They heard how I had left the captain on the island, naked and with no food, and begged me on their knees to send for him. I told them not to bother me, for that was the way to punish robbers and enemies of the Christians; let them be thankful I had not hanged him.

_____

The Life of Captain Alonso de Contreras, Knight of the Military Order of St. John, Native of Madrid, Written by Himself (1582–1633). Translated by Catherine A. Phillips. New York: Alfred A. Knopf, 1926, pp. 64–67.

Doc. 12: *European Renegade and Corsair John Ward*

In the early seventeenth century, John Ward was the most notorious English pirate operating in the Mediterranean. Born in 1553 at Faversham, Kent, he was first a fisherman and then went into the royal navy, which he deserted to become a Mediterranean corsair. By 1606 he commanded a band of roughly five hundred men that attacked Dutch, Venetian, and even English ships. Ward, who was one of the first known pirates to have been elected by his crew as captain, became a Muslim taking the name Yasuf Raïs. He lived out the rest of his life as a corsair in Tunis, dying in the plague of 1623 at the age of seventy. The excerpt below comes from the earliest pamphlet written about John Ward. The author, Andrew Barker, had been held as a prisoner in Tunis, having been captured by Ward's compatriot, William Graves. Barker gives a lively depiction of a loathsome character, presented in the colorfully arcane language of seventeenth-century seafarers. Such depictions helped to create the stereotypical images of pirates that we still hold today. Despite the somewhat heroic portrayal of Ward, Barker makes clear that he was not only a terrible villain but also an appalling sinner, who swore, drank, and gambled, as well as colluded with Infidels in robbing Christians. What is more, Ward and his men are portrayed as incorrigible sodomites. Barker's booklet was published in 1609, when Ward was in his prime.

This *Ward*, who now hath atchieved to himselfe, the title of Captaine, whose desperate actions hath caused terrour to travellors by Sea, and whose name hath bred feare in the Marchants at home. In the last yeare of her late Majesties raigne [i.e., Queen Elizabeth], was resident, and had his dwelling, (as by my own knowledge I can

certifie) in the West countrie at the haven Towne of *Plimouth*, a fellow, poore, base, and of no esteeme, one as tattered in cloathes, as
he was ragged in conditions, the good past, that he could boast of
himselfe, might bee, that hee was borne in a Towne called *Feversham*
in Kent, and there lived as a poore fisherman, and the vertue present, that he durst talke of was, he had abiding in *Plimouth*, wherfore
a while keeping house, although I have never heard that he paid his
rent, all the day you should hardly faile but finde him in an ale-
house: but bee sure to have him drunke at home at night. Othes
were almost as ordinarie with him as words, so that hee seldome
spake a sentence, but one was a silable, hee would sit melancholy,
speake doggedly, curse the time, repine at other mens good fortunes, and complaine of the hard crosses attended his owne.

* * *

It at last so happened, that in the beginning of the Kings raigne
[i.e., James I], hee found meanes to bee imployed for service, in
a small ship of his majesties, commoly called by the name of the
Lions Whelpe, in which imployment, persisting as before, in his
melancholy disposition, not contented, with that good and honest
meanes was allowed him[.] * * * But having new reaches working
in his braine, he one day selected out a choice crew, but of such,
whose dispositions he perceived were as untoward as his owne,
when the poison of his heart disgorged it selfe thus.

My mates, quoth he, whats to be done? heres a scurvy world, and
as scurvily we live in't, we feede here upon the water, on the kings
salt beefe, without ere a penie to buy us bissell when we come a
shore, heres brine, meat good for ravening stomacks, but wheres
your brim cup, and your full carouse that can make a merrie heart?
* * * O blood what would you have me say, where are the daies that
have beene, and the seasons that wee have seene, when we might
sing, sweare, drinke, drab, and kill men as freely, as your *Cake-
makers* doe flies? when we might doe what we list, and the Law
would beare us out int [in it?], nay when we might lawfully doe
that, we shall bee hangd for and we doe now, when the whole Sea
was our *Empire*, where we robd at will, and the world but our garden where we walked for sport[.]

* * *

[After deserting and gathering a gang, Ward and his men set out to rob the boat of a wealthy gentleman. But not finding any valuables aboard they stole the boat and set off on their pirating venture, which soon brought them to the corsair stronghold of Tunis.]

Where with small suit to the *King* [of Tunis], in respect hee [Ward] brought Marchandise with him, beneficiall to the state, hee had leave, their to find safe harbouring for himselfe, his ships and followers, where having made sale of his Commodities, and presented diverse acceptable presents to the *King of Tunis*, * * * and been his only supporter in all his disseignes, and upon whose promised favour and furtherance *Ward* growing bould, he was at length a suter to the *King*, that he might be received as his *subject*, or if not so, yet at all times, either in adversity or proseperitie, himselfe and what the Sea could yeeld him, might be ever *sanctuaried* under his Princely protection, and in recompence thereof, he vowed, hee would for ever after, become a foe to all *Christians*[.] * * * He puts forth from *Tunis*, and proceeded downe to the bottome of the *Straights*, where he hovered not long before hee tooke a small *Argosie*,[1] of the burden of six hundred *Tunnes*. In the same action also, he tooke a Ship of two hundred *Tunnes*, which he afterward named *The little John*, and armed her with foure and twenty peeces of *Ordinance*. Hee then surprised also the *Mattalena*, a *French Ship*, who came from *Alexandria* with rich *Commodities*.

* * *

Now concerning my knowledge in these *Proceedings*, they were all of them, and each particular delivered mee by *Graves*, who tooke mee *Prisoner*, and every circumstance thereof resolved mee at full, by divers others, whom I had severall conference withall. As also that they were above two hundred *Englishmen*, good *Souldiers*, and expert *Mariners*, when they proceeded forward to the *Gulf of Venice*. To the which voyage *incouraged* (saies *Graves*) we were foure well *mand*, and well *appointed* Ships, over whom *Captaine Ward* was our

[1] An argosie or argosy, a type of merchant vessel that originated in Ragusa, was in common use in Europe at the time.

worthy Generall, who being severed from us by a forcible *Tempest,* him-selfe in his small *Argosie,* having none but his *Fly-boat* with him, he met with a great *Argosie* of fourteene or fifteene hundred *Tunnes,* very richlie laden with *Venetian* goods, and who, by *Computation,* was esteemed to be worth *two millions* at the least, betwixt whom and him was such a *mercilesse* and *incredible fight,* as a man may compare is betweene those two *Tyrants,* the *remorselesse windes,* and the *resisting waters.* It was *long,* and it was *cruell,* it was *forcible,* and therefore feare-full: but in the end our *Captaine* had the *Sunshine*; he boorded her, subdued her, *chained* her men like *slaves,* and ceasd on her goods, as his lawfull prise, whom the whistling calme made musicke unto, ushering her and our *Generall* into *Tunis,* and whose bounty with his men, did there *triumph* with her *treasure.*

* * *

But as it is certaine, he that doth once accustome himselfe to sinne, is alwaies sitting upon *Cockatrice* egges, that bring foorth noth-ing but poisonous *effects*: so fares it with this *Ward,* and his whole company; and to approove, that goods ill gotten are most com-monlie worse spent, with this *Treasure,* which thus unjustly they had inriched themselves withall, they accustome their lives to all *disorder,* making their habit and carriage a shore, farre more detestable, and uncomely to be talked of, or by *Christianity* to be condemned and ab-horred, then their theeving at Sea, *swearing, drinking, dicing,* and the utmost enormities that are attended on by consuming riot, are the least of their *vices,* that can bee recited. Unlawfully are their goods got, and more ungodly are they consumed, in that they mix them-selves like brute beasts with their enemies of their Saviour: so that he that was a *Christian* in the morning, is bedfellow to a *Jew* at *night.* Nay sinne is growen to that *ranknesse* amongst them, through the fat-nesse of *Concupiscence* and *Covetousnesse,* that the *Jewes* hire out their *off-spring* to them as we doe *horses,* either by the *day* or by the *weeke*: * * * So then since that al men do know, it is a bad *fare* where noth-ing is bought, and a great many of the *Buiers,* I will leave their *Sodomie,* and the rest of their *crying sinnes* (which I feare their *Atheisme* hath led them into) to the *Judgement* of the *Just Revenger,* and not give them to be talked of further by my pen. Only for *Ward,* he lives there in *Tunis,* in a most princely and *magnificent* state. His *apparel* both curious and costly, his diet sumptuous, and his followers seriously observing and obeying his will. Hee hath two *Cookes* that dresse and prepare his diet for him, and his taster before he eats. I doe not know any Peere in *England* that beares up his port in more dignitie, nor hath his Attendants more obsequious unto him.

Andrew Barker, *A True and Certaine Report of the Beginning, Proceedings, Overthrowes and now present Estate of Captaine Ward and Danseker, the two late famous Pirates: from their first setting foorth to this present time.* London: Printed by William Hall, and are to be sold by John Helme at the shop in S. Dunstans Church-yard, 1609. Huntington Library, Rare Books Collection.

Doc. 13: *John Foss' Captivity in Algiers, 1793–96*

John Foss was a sailor aboard the merchant vessel Polly *when his ship was attacked and seized by Barbary corsairs on October 10, 1793. His ship was taken as a prize to Algiers and the crew was put into slavery. During the time of his captivity, which lasted some three years, another ten American vessels had been seized by corsairs, bringing the total number of American captives to 119. As negotiations for their release continued, Foss and the other prisoners worked as slaves building a breakwater or mole in the harbor at Algiers, as dockhands, or as oarsmen aboard corsair ships. Finally in the summer of 1796 the Americans signed a treaty with Algiers and the prisoners were redeemed. All told, the cost of the treaty, annual tribute, vessels and naval stores, and "gifts" to the Algerian rulers amounted to about one million dollars, approximately one-sixth of the federal budget. The following excerpt comes from Foss' recollections, published in 1798, of his harrowing experiences in captivity as a slave.*

[W]e arrived at Algiers, on Friday the 1st. of November [1793].

After they [i.e., the corsairs] had brought their vessel to an anchor in the roads, they hoisted out their boats and ordered us to embark, and to lay ourselves down in the bottom of the boat: And having obeyed their commands, we were rowed on shore, and landed, amidst the shouts and huzzas, of thousands of malicious barbarians. We were conducted to the Dey's [governor's] palace, by a guard, and as we passed through the streets, our ears were stunned with the shouts, clapping of hands, and other acclamations of joy from the inhabitants, thanking God for their great success, and victories over so many Christian dogs, and unbelievers, which is the appellation they generally give to all christians. On our arrival at the gates of the Palace, we were received by another guard, and conducted before the Dey, who after taking a view of us, told us he had sent several times to our Government, entreating them, to negociate with him for a peace, and had never received any satisfactory answer from them. And that he was determined, never to make a peace with the United States, (in his reign) as they had so often neglected his requests, and treated him with disdain, adding "now I have got you, you Christian dogs, you shall eat stones." * * *

After condoling our hapless fate, for a considerable time; a French priest[1] came to us and enquired, if any among us understood the French language, and was answered in the affirmative. After conversing sometime with the person who spoke French, he left us, and told us he should return in a few minutes. About half an hour afterwards he returned, and two moors with him, who brought two baskets full of white bread, and he gave each man, a loaf weighing nearly a pound, which was a very delicious meal for us, we having eaten nothing during the day, it now being about 4 o'clock in the afternoon. * * * [A little after 5 o'clock] we heard a man shouting out in a most terrible manner, and not understanding his language, made it sound more terrible.—We were immediately informed by a man, who understood the English language, that all of us (Americans) must appear in the third gallery.—We made all haste up, we possibly could, and as we entered the gallery, we passed one at a time, through a narrow door, on one side of which stood a task-master, and on the other side a Christian slave. The former had a large stick in his hand, and the latter a book, in which was written the names of all the Christian captives in that prison. The Christian asked each man his name, and then wrote it in the book, and as we passed, the Turk gave each man a small bundle. On examining it, we found it contained a blanket, a capoot, (which is a sort of jacket with a head,) a waist-coat, made something like a frock, to draw on over the head, it not being open at the belly, a shirt, with neither collar or wrist-bands, a pair of Trowsers,

---

[1]Barbary rulers allowed Catholic priests of various redemptionist orders to minister to Christian slaves in captivity. The priests fed and cared for sick prisoners and also helped negotiate ransoms for release.

made somewhat like a womans petticoat, (with this difference,) the bottom being sewed up, and two holes to put the legs through, and a pair of slippers. There was neither button, or button-hole in the whole suit. Such a suit excepting the blanket, of which they never get but one, is given to each captive once a year.

* * *

Soon after we received the above mentioned bundle, we were again called into the third gallery, and passed in the same manner as before, and having our names called by the clerk we passed the task master, and received each man a small loaf of very black, sour-bread weighing about three ounces and a half, which we ate, although it was not so delicious as the bread we received from the french priest. Having finished our supper, we lay down upon the stone floor, and went to sleep, and made ourselves as comfortable, as we could, having neither bed, nor beding, except the blanket before mentioned but being very much fatigued, we slept tolerably well until about three o'clock, when we were alarmed with a terrible shouting, as before, and were all ordered to go down into the lower part of the prison. When we arrived there, they put a chain on each man's leg, reaching up to the shoulder, and weighing about 25 or 40 lb. This done, it now being day break—Saturday the 2d. Nov. we were all driven out of the Bagnio [prison], and from thence to the marine, where I experienced the hardest days work, I ever underwent before. * * *

At day break in the morning, the Prison-keeper calls all the slaves out to go to work, and at the door of the Bagnio they are met by the *Guardians* or task-masters (who have their orders from the *Guardian Bachi*, who is the master of all the slaves that belong to the Regency) and we are conducted to whatever place he has directed.

The greatest part of their work, is blowing rocks in the Mountains. While some are drilling the holes, others are diging the earth off those rocks, which are under it, and others carrying away the dirt in baskets. When the rocks are blowed, they take such as will answer their purpose: (Rocks less than twenty Tons weight, will not serve.) Many are hauled by the slaves, two miles distance, which weigh forty tons. They roll them to the bottom of the mountain, where is a convenient place to put them on a sled, from thence they

FIGURE 12
Christian Slaves in Barbary (David Cordingly, ed., *Pirates*. Atlanta: Turner Publishers, 1996.)

are hauled to a quay [wharf], about two miles distant, and left. Those rolled down the mountain are left at the bottom, until Friday, (which is their Mahometan Sabbath,) on which day all the christian slaves belonging to the Regency, are driven out to haul them to the Quay. At day light in the morning they pass through the gates of the city, and arrive at the bottom of the mountain, sometime before sunrise. On their arrival, they are divided by the task-masters, into different gangs, and each gang has one sled. They must haul as many in a day as the task-masters think proper, and are treated with additional rigor and severity on this day. For the drivers being anxious to have as many hauled as possible, (because the number they haul must be reported to the Dey.)—they are continually beating the slaves with their sticks, and goading them with its end, in which is a small spear, not unlike an ox goad, among our farmers. If anyone chance to faint, and fall down with fatigue, they generally beat them until they are able to rise again. The most Tyrannical guardian, or task-master, we had, during my captivity, was known by the name of Sherief. This cruel villain never appeared to be in his element, except when he was cruelly punishing some Christian captive.

* * *

At night when they have done hauling, all hands are called together, and have their names called by the Clerk, and every one must pass the Guardian Bachi, as his name is called. After they have done calling, and find that none are missing they are driven by the task-masters, into the city, and then left to go to the Bagnio, by themselves, and must appear there within half an hour after they must enter gates of the city. The roll is called every night in the prison, a few minutes before the gates are locked. If any one neglects his call, he is immediately put into irons hands and feet, and then chained to a pillar, where he must remain until morning. Then the irons are taken from his feet, and he is driven before a task-master, to the marine, and the Vigilhadge, (who is the Minister of the marine) orders what punishment he thinks proper, which is immediately inflicted, by the task-masters. He commonly orders 150, or 200 Bastinadoes [floggings]. The manner of inflicting this punishment is as follows, the person is laid upon his face, with his hands in irons behind him and his legs lashed together with a rope.—One task-master holds down his head and another his legs, while two others inflict the punishment upon his breech, with sticks, some what larger than an ox goad. After he has received one half in this manner, they lash his ancles to a pole, and two Turks lift the pole up, and hold it in such a manner, as brings the soles of his feet upward, and the remainder of his punishment, he receives upon the soles of his feet. Then he is released from his bands, and obliged to go directly to work, among the rest of his fellow slaves. There is several other punishments, for the christian captives, for capital offences. Sometimes they are burned, or rather roasted alive. At other times they are impaled. This is done by placing the criminal upon a sharp iron stake, and thrusting it up his posteriors, by his back bone 'till it appears at the back of his neck. For being found with a Mahometan woman he is beheaded, and the woman, is put into a sack and carried about a mile at sea, and thrown overboard with a sufficient quantity of rocks, (or a bomb) to sink her. For suspicion of being with them the slave is castrated, and the woman bastinadoed.

* * *

I mentioned before, that on Friday, all the slaves work in the mountains, but on other days only a part of them work there. They have commonly a part of the captives at work in the marine. When they work in the marine, they have different kinds of employ. Sometimes they are cleaning the corsairs [ships], and fitting them for sea. At other times they are striping them, and hauling them up, discharging the prizes, cleaning the harbor, bringing those large rocks before mentioned, from the quay, on board a large flat bottomed kind of vessel which, they call a Puntoon, discharging them at back of the mole,[2] with the help of wheels. * * *

When their prizes are discharged, their cargo must be all carried into the city, and stowed in Magazines, so that some part of the slaves are constantly carrying hogsheads of sugar, pipes of wine, casks of nails, cannon, &c. They work from day break, in the morning, until a certain hour in the afternoon, (which they call Laza)

[2] A mole is a man made embankment of stone or masonry used to protect a harbor from storms, thereby sheltering ships at anchor.

which is just half an hour before sunset, summer and winter. At which time they hoist a white flag upon the mosques, to denote that it is the hour of prayer, it being contrary to their religion to have a bell sound among them.

All the slaves at this hour, are ordered to leave work and go up to the gate, called Babazia, which is the marine gate, and before they can pass, they are searched by the task-masters, to prevent their stealing any thing from the Regency, and if they are found with any thing, (except a few chips,) they do not escape punishment.

I have known a slave to receive 100 bastinadoes for being found with three board nails.

* * *

Perhaps you may think what I have already told you would not be augmented with additional severity, but alas, this is not all. The Bagnio in which they sleep, is built with several Galleries, one above another, in each gallery is several small rooms, where the slaves sleep. And they must pay a certain sum, every moon to the Guardian Bachi, or sleep in the open Bagnio, where they have nothing but the firmament to cover them. On the evening after the moon changes, the keeper of the Bagnio calls out for all hands to pay for their rooms. And if any one that has slept in a room during the moon, has not procured the money, and cannot pay it down, his hands are put into irons behind him, and his legs chained to a pillar every night, until the money is paid. And those miserable objects are commonly relieved by the rest of their fellow sufferers. Some of the slaves are allowed a small pittance from their country, which enables them to pay this demand. Others are mechanics and work at their trade in the night, to procure this sum, and others get it by theft, tho' they often hazzard their lives by so doing; and many are obliged to sleep every night upon the cold stones with nothing but the heavens to cover them, for want of money to pay this tribute.

John Foss, *A Journal, of the Captivity and Sufferings of John Foss; several years a prisoner in Algiers: Together with some account of the treatment of Christian slaves when sick:—and observations on the manners and customs of the Algerines.* Newburyport, MA: A. March, 1798. New York Public Library, Rare Books Division.

Pirates of the South China Coast

Doc. 14: *Cases of Wakō Piracy in Sixteenth-Century China*

Although the so-called wakō (wokou) disturbances began as early as the thir-teenth century when Japanese raiders plundered the coast of Korea, it was not until the middle of the sixteenth century, during the Chinese Ming dynasty (1368–1644), that wakō piracy became a serious problem in South China. By that time wakō bands consisted not only of Japanese but also Chinese and other foreign pirates, misfits, and renegades. The three selections below represent a cross-section of evidence from Japanese and Chinese sources concerning the ori-gins, development, and workings of wakō pirates in sixteenth-century China. The first document, purportedly written by a Japanese pirate in the 1570s, illustrates the wide scope of pirate activities both in Chinese and Southeast Asian waters. The second case, which comes from the official Ming imperial court record, describes how illicit trading could escalate into piracy and how wealthy Chinese families and merchants became involved with Japanese pirates. The last document briefly describes the career of the Chinese merchant-pirate, Hong Dizhen.

1. Excerpts from the *Memoirs of Sato Shinen* [*Sato Shinen no shuki*]:
  During the Eisho and Taiei eras [1504–1527] several warriors . . . from islands . . . off the coast of Iyo banded together and crossed the ocean to foreign lands, where they operated as pirates and became wealthy. Murakami Zusho, the lord of Noshima, was selected as their leader. The pirates pillaged coastal towns and seized all kinds of things, making themselves rich. They operated along the coast of China . . . , and among the islands of southeast as far as the Philippines, Borneo, and Bali. For several years they continued these forays. . . . In time ronins [masterless samurai], fishermen, scoundrels, and others from the Kyushu-Shikoku area joined the pirate bands, and gradually their size increased from eight to nine hundred to over a thousand men. Consequently, all the islands of the southwestern seas were harassed by pirates. Even Ming China feared them, and as a result sent out her huge armies

[to drive them away]. China also strengthened her coastal defences. It was at this time that the pirates came to be known as Wakō. . . .

Iida Koichiro of Oshima in the province of Iyo and Kitaura Kanjuro of Momojima in the province of Bingo were the first [pirate leaders] to sail to foreign lands, pillage the coastal villages, steal property and enrich their families. It is said that at first the two leaders had only fifty or sixty men under them, but with each raid their profits mounted considerably and, as a result, the bands became larger and more powerful.

In foreign countries soldiers were drawn up to guard the coast against our raids. Consequently, we increased our military strength. If we could not destroy the armies guarding the coast, we could gain no profit. Therefore, before setting sail we made complete preparations for engaging such armies in battle. In regard to these preparations Wu and Song[1] had a large number of guns and it became necessary to take proper countermeasures. Toward the end of the Tembun era [1554] we adopted the use of guns, which increased our military strength and enlarged the size of the pirate bands. In 1555 the number of men in the seven groups reached a total of more than 1,000. Each ship was loaded with 700 koku[2] of rice. There were eight or nine main vessels, the best of which were called Hagaibune. . . . In 1563 our seven bands totaling 1,300 men, attacked Pinghai[3] in Ming China. . . . We had one hundred and thirty-seven vessels of various sizes. . . . The total number of pirates of all classes reached the figure of 1,352 men, plus 60 fishermen and the like who made up the crew. Of the above two or three hundred Chinese pirates had joined our ranks. . . .

2. Excerpts from *The Veritable Records of the Emperor Shizong of the Ming Dynasty* [*Ming Shizong shilu*], dated July 28, 1549:

As we understand, the affairs of the coast originated from our treacherous traders Wang Zhi, Xu Hai, and others who often went out to sea unlawfully, carrying Chinese money and commodities

---

[1] The names Wu and Song refer to modern Jiangsu and Zhejiang provinces in coastal South China.

[2] One *koku* was equivalent to about 4.96 bushels.

[3] In the Ming dynasty, Pinghai was a fortified guardpost on the coast in Xinghua prefecture, Fujian province.

and trading with barbarian traders [in Japan and Southeast Asia]. All this was sponsored by a Xie family of Youyao [in Zhejiang province]. After some time the Xie family withheld some payments. The treacherous people pressed them for it. Figuring that they had owed too much to repay, the Xie family threatened them saying that they would inform the authorities on them. Being resentful and afraid, the treacherous men gathered their followers and the barbarian traders together and plundered the Xie family at night. They set fire to the living quarters, killed several men and women and plundered recklessly before they went away. Fearfully and hurriedly, the magistrate reported to his superiors, saying that the *wokou* had invaded. The governor, [Zhu] Wan,[4] issued orders to have the robbers arrested at once. [He] also ordered that those coastal people who had had intercourse with barbarians should come forward to confess their guilt and to inform on one another. Consequently, the people were thrown into a panic: they informed on one another or falsely accused the innocent. For fear that the government troops would search and arrest them, the treacherous elements, therefore, allied themselves with the island barbarians [i.e., the Japanese] and the notorious pirates at sea. Wherever they went, they plundered; taking advantage of the seasonal winds and tides, they went ashore. They often assumed the name of *wokou*, but in fact genuine Japanese *wokou* were not many. At that time the coast was inured to peace for a long time and people were not familiar with warfare. As soon as they heard about the coming of the pirates, they all fled like birds or quadrupeds leaving behind vacant houses and buildings. When government troops fought them, the troops, overawed by their reputation, collapsed running [for their lives]. [The trouble] spread to the Fujian waters and the regions between Zhejiang and Zhi.[5] Troops were deployed [from other parts of the empire], taxes were increased, the whole country was disturbed and the Court was kept busy and worried. It was like this for six or seven years. Only after the resources of the southeast were almost exhausted were

[4] Zhu Wan was appointed by the emperor as governor of Zhejiang province specifically to deal with the problems of piracy. His aggressive measures caused resentment among many powerful coastal families who had vested interests in the illegal trade. As a result, he was dismissed from office and in 1550 committed suicide.

[5] *Zhi* was a Ming term for modern Jiangsu and parts of Anhui provinces.

they barely overcome. Insignificant, indeed, was the origin of all these troubles.

3. Excerpts from the *Gazetteer of Zhangzhou Prefecture* [*Zhangzhou fuzhi*] of 1878:

[Hong Dizhen] was at first only engaged in trading. In the 34th and 35th years of the Jiajing reign [1555 and 1556] he came with some wealthy Japanese barbarians and anchored his ships at Nan'ao [an island bordering on Fujian and Guangdong]. He gained amply and henceforth came yearly. He made a huge fortune. There was still no evidence of his inducing the Japanese to engage in piracy. Sometimes when some Chinese were kidnapped or captured by *wokou*, he paid the ransom for them and sent them back [home]. People had high regard for him. In 1558 he came to Wuyu [an island south of Amoy]. All the young people of bad character went to him with supplies and they went in succession interminably. The authorities could not stop this and sent out eight-oar boats[6] for their arrest and could not get even a single one. They just seized ordinary trading ships and had them sent over to the authorities. Accordingly, [Hong] Dizhen began to hold the authorities in contempt. [They] also arrested and imprisoned his relatives. From then on, Dizhen made up his mind and allied with the *wokou* to start trouble. . . .

Kwan-wai So, *Japanese Piracy in Ming China During the 16th Century*. East Lansing: Michigan State University Press, 1975, pp. 15–16, 24–25, 34–35. For the purpose of consistency the Editor has changed the spelling of Chinese words to the *pinyin* transliteration system.

Doc. 15: *The Pirate Zheng Zhilong*

Zheng Zhilong (1604–1661), who was known to foreigners as Nicholas Iquan, lived during the turbulent transition between the Ming and Qing dynasties. Married to a Japanese woman, his early career was that of a merchant and pirate in the competitive overseas trade between China and Japan. Eliminating

---

[6] A common Chinese vessel used in shallow coastal waters by smugglers, pirates, and coast guards.

FIGURE 13
An Eight-Oar Boat (*Gujin tushu jicheng*, 1884.)

his rivalries one by one, he gradually erected a vast maritime empire that domi-
nated the trade of southern China and Southeast Asia. After surrendering to the
Ming dynasty in 1628, he continued to increase his power under the aegis of
the official military establishment, eventually rising to the position of grand
admiral. It was said that no ships could sail without his permission. He levied
protection fees on merchant junks and plundered those that refused to pay. Even
a number of high-ranking officials were on his payroll. However, when it

became apparent that the Manchu founders of the Qing dynasty were unstoppable, Zheng Zhilong betrayed his Ming benefactors and surrendered in 1646 to the new rulers. Unfortunately, he was put under house arrest until his execution in 1661. The following excerpt from a literatus named Shao Tingcai (1648–1711) describes Zheng Zhilong's career during the height of his power in the 1620s to 1640s.

Zheng Zhilong, whose style (*zi*) was Flying Yellow (Fei Huang),[1] came from Nan'an, Fujian. His father, named Shaozu, was a clerk in the yamen treasury in Quanzhou prefecture. When Zhilong was ten years old, while out playing, he accidentally hit the prefect on his head with a rock. He was grabbed and brought before the court, but the prefect taking note of the lad's handsome features dismissed the charges, telling Zhilong that one day "you will prosper and become a high-ranking official." Not many years later, he wandered off to sea where he joined up with Yan Zhenquan's gang and became a pirate. After Zhenquan died, Zhilong became chief. Not long afterwards when there was a severe famine in southern Fujian, Zhilong seized several private merchant junks, robbed them of their rice, and fed the hungry famine victims. As a result, his ranks swelled to several tens of thousands.[2] In the sixth lunar month of 1627, he pillaged the military post at Tongshan. * * * Zhilong did not allow his men to indiscriminately kill civilians and soldiers in the towns he raided, but only took what he needed. In 1628, * * * after the Ming court allowed Zhilong to surrender, he bribed high-ranking officials with exotic gifts in order to be rewarded an admiral's commission. Later on, as ordered by the government, he had his former pirate comrades, Liu Xiang, Li Kueiqi, and others put to death. Now the last of his comrades to remain alive, Zhilong was the only one able to grab up the profits of the South China Sea [trade]. All of the merchant junks passing through the South China Sea had to have Zhilong's safe-conduct pass. Therefore, all of the outlaws and rabble in the whole region pledged allegiance to him

---

[1] *Zi* referred to the name or style a man took after he reached the age of twenty. Zheng's style, Flying Yellow, was taken from the Chinese proverb *feihuang tengda*, "to make rapid advances in one's career."

[2] This number is much inflated; his followers probably numbered only several thousands.

and came under his control. Later, following the emperor's command, he waged war against the Red Barbarians [i.e., the Dutch], for which he was promoted to grand admiral. He now became as powerful as a royal descendent. * * * [At the height of his power in the mid-1640s] he built a mansion in the town of Anping, fifty *li*[3] from Quanzhou. He built a moat and wall around the entire town, and [a channel] that allowed sea-going junks to sail right up to his boudoir. He kept all his treasure, weapons, and ammunition there in his mansion, and surrounded himself with skillful people who managed his property and invested his money. He kept an office in Fuzhou, [the provincial capital] where even the highest-ranking officials had to bow to him.

Shao Tingcai, *Dongnan jishi* [*A record of events in the southeast*]. Published in the Guangxu reign (1875–1908). Translation by Lanshin Chang.

Doc. 16: *Depositions in the Case of He Xing's Gang, 1782*

In this routine memorial the governor of Guangdong province, Debao, reported to the throne a case of piracy along the Sino-Vietnamese border that occurred in 1782. The victim was a merchant named Tong Shengru who had gone to the black market town of Giang Binh to trade, perhaps somewhat clandestinely. He testified that in the summer of that year a gang of pirates had robbed the vessel he had hired from Weng Panda, and on which they were both traveling. He Xing's band was a typical small ad hoc gang composed of impoverished fishermen and sailors who regularly alternated between legitimate work and crime in earning their livings. Shortly after the incident several of the pirates were apprehended and brought to trial. He Xing and most of the other gang members escaped. What follows are excerpts from the depositions of the victims Tong Shengru and Weng Panda and then the confession of a reluctant pirate named Wang Yade.

I, an unassuming subject, [Tong Shengru] originally came from Jiaying Subprefecture and opened a cosmetics shop in Hengye village in a placc called Neighing Horse Hamlet (Masishe). On the ninth

------

[3] One *li* is equivalent to 1,890 feet.

day of the sixth lunar month of this year (1782), I hired Weng Panda's boat to transport perfumes and powders to Giang Binh to sell. On the thirteenth day [after completing my business transactions] in Giang Binh I collected my money and goods to return to my shop. That night on the ocean at a place known as Flowing Water (Lizhu) a boatload of pirates robbed us. Their boat suddenly heaved along side us and then, like a swam of hornets, they boarded our vessel grabbing money and goods and then fleeing. The next morning we repaired to Lizhang where we began searching everywhere for the culprits. On the twentieth day we spotted the pirate boat in Zhangshan harbor. [After reporting the incident to] the local market head, together we apprehended two culprits, Li Xiang and Wang Yade. We also recovered some of our stolen property. The others had already gotten away. Afterwards, we turned the pirate boat over to the port authorities in Zhangshan.

* * *

[In his stolen property report, Tong Shengru listed the following items:] 63 strings of cash each having 600 coins; 3,000 dried betel nuts; two boxes of gilded auspicious paper ingots;[1] one iron cooking wok; one basket for holding cooked rice; 15 pecks[2] of rice; seven catties[3] of raw tobacco; two catties of fresh betel nuts; two hand towels; three paper fans; twenty writing brushes; one sickle; one cloth bundle holding four sets of clothing, a money purse, and an umbrella.

* * *

[Governor Debao's memorial continued:] In the possession of the two culprits, Li Xiang and Wang Yade, were found a box of gilded auspicious paper ingots, an iron wok, an umbrella, and a large colored cloth bundle containing one red cloth bag, two compasses, a pair of cotton socks, an old black silk scarf, a pair of leather shoes, a pair of scissors, a ruler; there was also a chest

---

[1] This was mock ingots of tinfoil paper, commonly referred to in English as "Mongol Ingots" (*yuanbao*), which were burned as offerings to Chinese deities.

[2] One peck (*dou*) approximated 316 cubic inches by volume or roughly 13.3 pounds by weight.

[3] One catty (*jin*) equaled 1.3 pounds.

containing an old cloth sack, an old green cotton kerchief, a black pair of pants, a bag of rags; and another black cloth bundle containing an old black cotton kerchief, an old black cotton coat, and a pair of hemp-cloth pants.

* * *

I, your humble subject, [Weng Panda] come from Hepu County. I transport people and goods on my boat for a living. On the ninth day of the sixth lunar month of 1782, Tong Shengru hired me to transport him and his perfumes and powders from his store in Hengye village to Giang Binh. We agreed that he would pay me 21 copper cash (*wen*) for my service. We arrived in Giang Binh on the evening of the twelfth. My passenger [Tong] sold his perfumes and powders, and the next day we began the return trip laden with the goods that he had bought. That night near Lizhu harbor we anchored for the night. Around midnight all of a sudden a boatload of robbers came along side us. When me and Tong screamed out, the robbers pelted us with stones. At first two robbers grabbed knifes and boarded my boat and threatened us to keep quiet. After that three or four of the robbers jumped aboard. We could see that the robbers were ruthless and cruel so none of us dared to move or say a word. They threw me, my crew and passenger into the ship's hold, and they continued to plunder the vessel and transfer the money and goods to their boat. Afterwards they sailed away. Because it was dark and we were afraid we didn't chase after them. But at the time I was able to make out some peculiar markings on their boat, which I told to Tong. The next morning we sailed back into the harbor and looked everywhere for the robbers' boat. On the twentieth I spotted it anchored at Zhangshan. Afterwards, we went together with the market head to the robbers' boat and apprehended Li Xing and Wang Yade, as well as some of the stolen items. Then we handed the culprits over to the local authorities.

* * *

I, your humble subject, [Wang Yade] come from Hepu County. I am 21 years old. I make my living as a sailor. I know Li Xing very well. This year [1782], early in the sixth lunar month, the cost of rice was very high, and so I went to Giang Binh to look for some work. On the tenth day of that month I ran into Li Xing and he took me to see He Xing who was looking to hire sailors on his boat. He agreed to pay me 150 cash[4] each month in wages. Aboard He's boat there were three other sailors and a helmsman, so that the total, including the skipper, Li Xing, and me, was seven men. On the afternoon of the thirteenth, He Xing went to the market to find us a job, but he returned to tell us that there was no work anywhere in that port. What is more we were out of rice to eat. He told us that while at the market he had heard that Weng Panda's boat had on board a passenger named Tong who had money and goods and was about to return to his store in Hengye village. He said why don't we go out to meet them on route at sea and rob them of their money and goods? How's that for a piece of work? Li Xing and the others all agreed, but this humble subject was afraid to join with them. He Xing cursed at me and said he would throw me overboard right then if I didn't agree. I didn't dare refuse and so went along with them. They set off and that evening we awaited our prey at a place offshore near Lizhu harbor. Around midnight Tong arrived and his boat anchored for the night. He Xing, Li Xing and the others pulled our boat up to his. But when they jumped aboard to rob Tong's boat, I hid myself in the stern afraid to come out. Afterwards He Xing and the others grabbed money and goods and brought them aboard our boat and we sailed off to a secluded spot in barbarian [i.e., Vietnamese] waters to split up the booty. I didn't dare take a share, but He Xing told me that since I went along with them and knew about the heist, if ever a word leaked out to anyone he would kill me. He then gave me 2,000 cash. I was afraid of him so I didn't refuse. On the twentieth we anchored at Zhangshan mart. He Xing and three others went ashore to buy food and provisions. Me, Li Xing, and Ge'er remained on board to watch things. We didn't know that the victim had already discovered our whereabouts and was on his way with the market head to arrest us. As

---

[4] About 1,000 cash equaled 1 Spanish silver dollar. At that time, 1 catty (1.3 pounds) of rice cost about 5 cash, and on the average a male Chinese ate 1 cattie of rice a day. Wages, therefore, provided a sailor only enough money to buy a day's worth of rice and not much else— barely enough for subsistence. Thus, the 2,000 cash Wang received as his share of the booty was an enormous sum of money.

soon as Ge'er saw them coming he jumped ashore and ran away. The victim and the others came aboard and nabbed Li Xing and me.

Xingke tiben [Routine Memorial], dated 11th day, 10th lunar month, 48th year of the Qianlong Emperor's reign (1783), First Historical Archives, Beijing. Translation by the Editor.

Doc. 17: *Cai Qian and Matron Cai Qian, early nineteenth century*

The following three accounts about Cai Qian and his wife, Matron Cai Qian, come from the local histories or gazetteers of three coastal counties in South China. Stories such as these are based on actual incidents as well as legends and hearsay. In the early nineteenth century Cai Qian and his wife were the two most notorious and powerful pirates operating in the waters between Fujian and Zhejiang provinces. Like Zheng Yi Sao and Maria Cobham, discussed by Jo Stanley in Part 3, Matron Cai Qian became a pirate only because of connections with her husband. On several occasions they invaded Taiwan not only for plunder but also—perhaps emulating Zheng Chenggong before them—to use the island as a base for their piratical raids. Cai Qian died in battle with the imperial navy in 1809, but it is uncertain how his wife died—some accounts say that she was murdered by her jealous husband, but it is more likely that she died fighting Qing soldiers in 1804 on one of the many raids on Taiwan.

---

1. Cai Qian was a native of Tongan county [in Fujian province]. He made his living as a cotton bower and later went to sea as a pirate. In the early years of the Jiaqing Emperor's reign (1796–1820) he had over a hundred ships. His wife was very brave and cunning. At that time there were other pirate chiefs, such as Zhu Fen, Zhang Bao, Phoenix Tail (Fengwei), Short Ox (Ainiu), Red Head (Hongtou), White Bottom (Baidi), and petty local gangs that complemented Cai's fleet. Everyone called Cai "Master of the Sea" (*da chuhai*). The three provinces of Fujian, Guangdong, and Zhejiang all suffered at his hands; there was nowhere he did not go. One time when [his fleet] anchored at Tiger Head Ocean (Hutou yang), somewhere south of Amoy and north of Tongshan, hun-

dreds of his men availed themselves of the night to rob six small
and large iron cannon from [the fort at] Dadan, killing the commander, Chen Fenggao, and five soldiers. * * * Cai desired to swal-
low up Taiwan and in 1800 he pillaged Luermen.[1] In 1804, he
raided Fengshan [on Taiwan]; Prefect Qin Bao defended Donggang but his wife was killed by cannon fire. In the fourth lunar
month of 1805, Cai again attacked Luermen. In the eleventh lunar
month he entered the harbor of Huwei [at the mouth of the Dan-
shui River], and captured Xinzhuang and Mengzha [Taipei].
Other ships raided Donggang and captured Fengshan, killing the
magistrate. They then returned to Luermen and laid siege to the
walled prefectural capital [at Tainan]. Cai sunk a large ship at
Luermen, thereby blocking the harbor to prevent other ships from
relieving the capital. With the support of local bandits, he assumed
the title "Magestic Warrior King" (weiwu wang), and gave out titles
and distributed seals and flags among his followers. * * * In the first
lunar month of the following year, Li Changgeng, commander of
the Qing provincial fleet, defeated Cai Qian [and drove him away
from Taiwan]. * * * In the fifth lunar month [1806] Cai joined up
with Zhu Fen and again raided Luermen [but they were defeated].
* * * In 1809, Cai Qian drowned at sea in a naval battle * * * off
the Zhejiang coast near Fish Mountain (Yushan).

2. In Yanting harbor [in Zhejiang province] there was a certain
beauty who, although married, enjoyed gallivanting about with
many men. Her husband couldn't stop her, so he sold her to a barber. One day when Cai Qian went ashore to have his hair groomed,
he noticed the barber's new wife. Overcome by her beauty he
immediately bought her for several tens of gold [coin]. After
becoming Cai Qian's wife, she used her skills to help him manage
his ships and control the pirates. She was very precise and organized in her methods. Whenever there was a battle she fought
bravely and no one could defeat her. The people living along the
coast all called her Matron Cai Qian.

3. Cai Qian and his wife both smoked opium. Once intoxicated
on the opium Cai Qian would open the ship's hold and take out
male captives to disembowel them. He'd cut open their chests, and

---

[1] Luermen was the port for Taiwan Prefecture, the city of Tainan today.

take out their livers to cook and eat.[2] He could eat as many as four livers in a day. His wife was a very brave and fierce fighter; she led several boats of female warriors (*niangzijun*). She kept men in her ship's hold and would take them out, selecting the handsome ones to satisfy her carnal pleasures. If captives begged for their lives she would let them go. Cai Qian dared not interfere or try to stop her. I heard this story from my father who heard it from his teacher, Wu Zhipu, who lived in Quanzhou during the Jiaqing reign, just a few years after Cai Qian had been killed.

Xiamen zhi [*Gazetteer of Amoy*], 1832 edition; *Pingyang xianzhi* [*Gazetteer of Pingyang county*], 1925 edition; and *Maxiang tingzhi* [*Gazetteer of Maxiang subprefecture*], 1893 edition. Translation by Lanshin Chang.

Doc. 18: *Imperial Edict Concerning the Problem of Piracy, 1803*

In the first decade of the nineteenth century Cai Qian was the most powerful pirate on the coast of Fujian, with operations extending into neighboring Zhejiang province and the island of Taiwan. His vast criminal syndicate was financed not only through robbery and kidnapping but also through a sophisticated protection racket that employed secret society members as well as government underlings and soldiers. Unscrupulous merchants on shore also collaborated with pirates. The whole system was highly institutionalized, with tribute being collected regularly on a semiannual or annual basis at "tax bureaus" where full-time bookkeepers kept account books and issued safe-conduct passes. In the edict below, as corruption became increasingly pervasive, the Jiaqing Emperor (1796–1820) instructed the governor of Fujian to carefully send out capable and trustworthy spies to infiltrate pirate and secret society organizations so as to capture the ringleaders. Overt military actions, the emperor believed, would be of no use.

---

[2] While this could be purely hearsay, there are genuine eyewitness accounts of other pirates practicing cannibalism and sacrificing humans out of revenge and hatred for their enemies and for the magico-religious powers to be derived from eating the hearts and livers of one's enemies.

I was informed recently that in Fujian pirates and secret society members are joint partners in crime. In port towns every merchant ship that goes overseas has to pay 400 [Spanish silver] dollars. Any ship returning from abroad has to pay double this amount. The fee is handed to Cai Qian. If this fee is paid, nothing will happen. Otherwise any unwilling merchant will lose both his fortune and his life. Furthermore, on land the number of secret society members is great. Even some of the clerks and runners in the government services are joining these societies [and also colluding with pirates]. The local authorities helplessly watch this growing trend, but do not dare to do anything about it. If this trend does not stop in time, it will result in great disaster. I therefore instruct you to investigate secretly. You should send capable men in your office to infiltrate into these societies by disguising themselves as merchants willing to cooperate, in order to discover the true identities of the ringleaders and their whereabouts. In this way, the ringleaders of these societies may be captured in one sweep. Once they are captured, they should be executed immediately. The lives of lower-ranking members, or members who were forced to join these societies, should be spared. If you can tackle several such cases in this way, people will be greatly impressed and may divert their minds towards better things. If we execute scores of criminals to save the lives of millions, how vast will be our merit! As for Cai Qian, he is a great and wicked pirate. As long as he remains, there will be no peace in our waters. I suspect that those who share the booty with Cai are mostly members of secret societies. The best way to conduct a secret investigation is to look around in the monasteries, flower boats [floating brothels], and opium dens. Then you can find clues and information. If you proclaim openly and send out troops to make arrests, this will simply drive the guilty ones into open revolt. Any open action against them not only will bring you no result, but also will cause immense damage to your investigation. Be careful and be secretive.

Shangyudang [Imperial edict record book], dated 13th day, 9th lunar month, 4th year of the Jiaqing Emperor's reign (1803). First Historical Archives, Beijing. Translation by the Editor.

Doc. 19: *Chinese Pirate Pact of 1805*

In 1805 seven of the most powerful pirate chieftains in Guangdong, including Zheng Yi (referred to as Zheng Wenxian in the document), came together and signed a pact, thereby formally establishing a loose confederation that numbered over 50,000 pirates. They made this agreement, not to guarantee egalitarianism and democracy aboard their vessels—as was the case among Western pirates (see Doc. 9)—but rather to bring law and order to the unruly gangs. For several years previous to this pact anarchy and fighting prevailed among the numerous bands of pirates. Specifically, the pact set out to regulate operating procedures among different fleets and gangs and to create a code of conduct among the pirates themselves. Harsh punishments were prescribed for violations of the agreement. Over the next two years the confederation had stabilized at six self-sustaining fleets or branches, each one designated by a separate colored banner, and this remained the situation until its collapse in 1810.

We the signatories to this pact—Zheng Wenxian, Mai Youjin, Wu Zhiqing, Li Xiangqing, Zheng Liutang, Guo Xiexian, and Liang Bao—have discussed it among ourselves and have openly agreed about the rules. If regulations are not harsh they will not be obeyed, and therefore trade will be harmed. Today we have achieved a great accomplishment by agreeing to join forces and making this pact. * * * No matter if the commands are big or small, or if the ships are far or near, everyone must obey these rules. * * *

The regulations are as follows:

1. We have agreed that our large and small seagoing vessels will be arranged in seven branches as Heaven (*Tian*), Earth (*Di*), Black (*Xuan*), Yellow (*Huang*), Universe (*Yu*), Cosmos (*Zhou*), and Vast (*Hong*). Each branch must record the nicknames of their commanders in a register. Every fast boat[1] must have its branch name and registration number written on the bow and must fly the branch's banner on its foremast. If the bow does not display the branch name and registration number or the foremast displays a banner with the wrong color, then that

---

[1] Fast boats were two-masted vessels commonly used for fishing and coasting. They were also a favorite among the pirates because they handled well both at sea and in coastal waters.

vessel and its weapons will be confiscated and the commander executed.

2. Each branch shall have its own name and number. If any [vessel] falsely displays another branch's name and banner, then as soon as it is discovered the vessel and its weapons will become the property of the whole group. [Because] the commander has intentionally cheated the whole group then the whole group will decide his fate.

3. If a fast boat disregards the regulations to stop and damage a vessel [with one of our safe conduct passes], and then sells its cargo or steals its money and clothes, the value of the loot must be estimated and [the victim] compensated. The offending vessel's weapons will be confiscated and the commander will be punished according to the circumstances of the case. If the offending vessel cannot pay the compensation then the amount will be deducted from its share [of the common fund].

4. Whenever attacking merchant junks [without passes], all of the captured cargo will become the property of the vessel that attacks it first. If others forcefully take it from the initial captors, the value of the prize must be estimated and the initial captor must be compensated with a sum double the original value. Anyone who disobeys this rule will be subject to attack from the entire group.

5. No matter which branch's fast boats stop a junk with a pass, those who witness the action and apprehend the culprits will be rewarded with 100 silver dollars. If any of our brothers is wounded in the action the entire group consents to their medical care. Moreover, the amount of compensation that the culprits must pay will be decided by the whole group. Those witnesses who do not come forward to take action [against the culprits] will be punished as accomplices.

6. If there are vessels that sail without permission to oceans and harbors to rob small trading boats and the money of merchants who have [safe conduct] passes, once they are captured by any of the branch's patrol boats, then the [culprits'] boat will be burned, their weapons confiscated, and their bosses executed.

7. If there are merchants on either land or sea who have been the enemies of any one of us, and who dare not hide themselves but continue to openly do business [with us], we must restrain our personal anger for the good of the entire group. We cannot use our power as a pretext to harm them on the grounds that they are our enemies or implicate their kith and kin as an excuse to kidnap them. Once such violations are discovered they will be punished for false implication.

8. If [the commander of a] flagship has something to discuss concerning the whole group then he should hoist a flag on his mainmast and the big bosses of each branch should come to confer. If a branch leader has an order to transmit to his fast boats, he should hoist a flag on the third mast, and all junks must assemble to listen to the orders. Those who do not assemble will be held in contempt and punished accordingly.

By order of our chief commander, [this pact] shall be copied and sent to each ship so as to be obeyed.

Heavenly Circle Reign, Yiqiu year, sixth lunar month [1805]
Written by Wu Shangde

Zhupi zouzhi [Palace Memorial], dated 22nd day, 11th lunar month, 10th year of the Jiaqing Emperor's reign (1805). First Historical Archives, Beijing. Translation by Lanshin Chang and the Editor.

Doc. 20: *A Chinese "Song of Ransom"*

The following poem, written at the start of the nineteenth century by a scholar who lived along the South China coast, vividly describes the plight of victims kidnapped by pirates. They abducted victims for ransom, to sell, or to work aboard ship as virtual slaves. Pirate chiefs grilled prisoners to assess their worth and determined the amount of ransom payments according to family background and ability to pay. Pirates normally released captives after ransoms were paid; in those cases, however, where they were not paid or did not meet the deadline, then the prisoners would lose a finger or ear or sometimes be killed. Besides monetary payments, pirates also demanded payments in food, opium, weapons, and naval stores.

Pirate ships at sea, a hundred or so in number,
North, east, south, and west wait for passing guests [i.e., victims].
In an encounter, the sounds of cannon fire shake the sky,
And countless pirates shouting in unison swarm on board.
Everyone turns pale and grows sick with fear,
As daggers fall white as snow,
They methodically loot cargo and seize passengers;
They feign furious anger at prisoners brought on board.
The captives scrape and bow on seeing the pirate chief.
The chief, his head wrapped in a red kerchief,
Interrogates both rich and poor, who beg for their lives;
The ransom for each is set at ten thousand or more in gold.
With a great shout, he orders paper and brush for carefully penned
    notes,
Demanding a hundred items to be delivered within ten days,
And should the deadline be missed, the hostages will be
    disemboweled.
Letters are sped off to their closest kin,
Who pawn clothing and personal belongings and beg for loans.
Concealing their bitterness, they think up ways to solve the problem,
And send people out to sea to make the exchange;
If only lives can be saved, why mention destitution.
Even commoners living along the coast,
Day after day, terror stricken, flee in all directions.
They sleep each night in caves deep in the mountains,
At daybreak they return to wrecked houses to fix their meals.
However, the pirates track down the cooking fires on shore;
Those who fail to escape in time are seized.
The elders are kept as hostages and their sons are set free
To quickly sell their oxen for less than half their value,
In tears they barter off their young sons for a handful of cash.
[Afterwards] the elders return to grieve for their broken families:
People gone and wealth exhausted, only four empty walls remain.
They do not die of cruelty or violence, but perish in poverty.

Thomas Chang, "Ts'ai Ch'ien, the Pirate King who Dominates the Seas: A Study of Coastal Piracy in China, 1795–1810," Ph.D. dissertation, University of Arizona, 1983, pp. 251–252. Translation modified by the Editor.

Doc. 21: *Narrative of Richard Glasspoole's Captivity, 1809*

Richard Glasspoole, who was a mate on the British East India Company ship
Marquis of Ely, *was abducted by pirates of the Red Banner fleet in the
waters off Macao on the morning of September 21, 1809. This was during
the height of the pirate disturbances in Guangdong. Glasspoole remained a prisoner among the pirates for over two months, during which time he was able to
closely observe their raiding operations, religious practices, treatment of women,
and daily lives and customs. For his release the pirates had originally demanded
70,000 dollars, but after tough negotiations the ransom was reduced to a payment of 4,200 dollars in cash, as well as two bales of scarlet cloth, two chests
of opium, two casks of gunpowder, and a telescope. In the following excerpt
Glasspoole describes a raiding expedition deep into the Canton Delta.*

Tuesday the 25th [of September], at day-light in the morning, the
[pirate] fleet, amounting to about five hundred sail of different
sizes, weighed, to proceed on their intended cruize up the rivers, to
levy contributions on the towns and villages. * * *

Wednesday the 26th, at day-light, we passed in sight of our ships
at anchor under the island of Chun Po. The chief then called me,
pointed to the ships, and told the interpreter to tell us to look at
them, for we should never see them again. About noon we entered
a river to the westward of the Bogue, three or four miles from the
entrance [of the Pearl River]. We passed a large town situated
on the side of a beautiful hill, which is tributary to the Ladrones
[pirates]; the inhabitants saluted them with songs as they passed.

The fleet now divided into two squadrons (the red and the
black)[1] and sailed up different branches of the river. At midnight
the division we were in anchored close to an immense hill, on the
top of which a number of fires were burning, which at day-light I
perceived proceeded from a Chinese camp. At the back of the hill
was a most beautiful town, surrounded by water, and embellished
with groves of orange-trees. The chop-house (custom-house) and a

---

[1] The red and the black banner fleets were the two most powerful fleets in the Guangdong
confederation, the former commanded by Zheng Yi Sao and Zhang Bao and the latter by
Guo Podai. The combined fleets had roughly 22,000 followers.

few cottages were immediately plundered, and burnt down; most of the inhabitants, however, escaped to the camp.

The Ladrones now prepared to attack the town with a formidable force, collected in row-boats from the different vessels. They sent a messenger to the town, demanding a tribute of ten thousand dollars annually, saying, if these terms were not complied with, they would land, destroy the town, and murder all the inhabitants; which they would certainly have done, had the town laid in a more advantageous situation for their purpose; but being placed out of the reach of their shot, they allowed them to come to terms. The inhabitants agreed to pay six thousand dollars, which they were, to collect by the time of our return down the river. * * *

October the 1st, the fleet weighed in the night, dropped by the tide up the river, and anchored very quietly before a town surrounded by a thick wood. Early in the morning the Ladrones assembled in row-boats, and landed; then gave a shout, and rushed into the town, sword in hand. The inhabitants fled to the adjacent hills, in numbers apparently superior to the Ladrones. We may easily imagine to ourselves the horror with which these miserable people must be seized, on being obliged to leave their homes, and every thing dear to them. It was a most melancholy sight to see women in tears, clasping their infants in their arms, and imploring mercy for them from those brutal robbers! The old and the sick, who were unable to fly, or to make resistance, were either made prisoners or most inhumanly butchered! The boats continued passing and repassing from the junks to the shore, in quick succession, laden with booty, and the men besmeared with blood! Two hundred and fifty women, and several children, were made prisoners, and sent on board different vessels. They were unable to escape with the men, owing to that abominable practice of cramping their feet [i.e., foot binding]: several of them were not able to move without assistance, in fact, they might all be said to totter, rather than walk. Twenty of these poor women were sent on board the vessel I was in; they were hauled on board by the hair, and treated in a most savage manner.

When the chief came on board, he questioned them respecting the circumstances of their friends, and demanded ransoms accordingly, from six thousand to six hundred dollars each. He ordered them a berth on deck, at the after part of the vessel, where they had nothing to shelter them from the weather, which at this time was very variable,—the days excessively hot, and the nights cold, with heavy rains. The town being plundered of every thing valuable, it was set on fire, and reduced to ashes by the morning. The fleet remained here three days, negotiating for the ransom of the prisoners, and plundering the fish-tanks and gardens. * * *

October the 5th, the fleet proceeded up another branch of the river, stopping at several small villages to receive tribute, which was generally paid in dollars, sugar and rice, with a few large pigs roasted whole, as presents for their joss (the idol they worship).[2] Every person on being ransomed is obliged to present him with a pig, or some fowls, which the priest[3] offers him with prayers; it remains before him a few hours, and is then divided amongst the crew. Nothing particular occurred 'till the 10th, except frequent skirmishes on shore between small parties of Ladrones and Chinese soldiers. They frequently obliged my men to go on shore, and fight with the muskets we had when taken, which did great execution, the Chinese principally using bows and arrows. They have matchlocks, but use them very unskilfully.

On the 10th, we formed a junction with the Black-squadron, and proceeded many miles up a wide and beautiful river, passing several ruins of villages that had been destroyed by the Black-squadron. On the 17th, the fleet anchored abreast four mud batteries, which defended a town, so entirely surrounded with wood that it was impossible to form any idea of its size. The weather was very hazy, with hard squalls of rain. The Ladrones remained perfectly quiet for two days. On the third day the forts commenced a brisk fire for several hours: the Ladrones did not return a single shot, but weighed in the night and dropped down the river.

The reasons they gave for not attacking the town, or returning the fire, were that Joss had not promised them success. They are very superstitious, and consult their idol on all occasions. If his omens are good, they will undertake the most daring enterprizes.

---

[2] *Joss* was a Chinese corruption of the Portuguese word *Dios* or God.

[3] Aboard most Chinese ships, including pirate vessels, there was a religious specialist who was a member of the crew and who had the daily job of burning incense and making offerings to the deities while at sea. This is the person that Glasspoole refers to as a priest.

The fleet now anchored opposite the ruins of the town where the women had been made prisoners. Here we remained five or six days, during which time about an hundred of the women were ransomed; the remainder were offered for sale amongst the Ladrones, for forty dollars each. The woman is considered the lawful wife of the purchaser, who would be put to death if he discarded her. Several of them leaped over-board and drowned themselves, rather than submit to such infamous degradation.

The fleet then weighed and made sail down the river, to receive the ransom from the town before-mentioned. As we passed the hill, they fired several shot at us, but without effect. The Ladrones were much exasperated, and determined to revenge themselves; they dropped out of reach of their shot, and anchored. Every junk sent about a hundred men each on shore, to cut paddy,[4] and destroy their orange-groves, which was most effectually performed for several miles down the river. During our stay here, they received information of nine boats lying up a creek, laden with paddy; boats were immediately dispatched after them.

Next morning these boats were brought to the fleet; ten or twelve men were taken in them. As these had made no resistance, the chief said he would allow them to become Ladrones, if they agreed to take the usual oaths before the Joss. Three or four of them refused to comply, for which they were punished in the following cruel manner: their hands were tied behind their back, a rope from the mast-head rove through their arms, and hoisted three or four feet from the deck, and five or six men flogged them with three rattans twisted together 'till they were apparently dead; then hoisted them up to the mast-head, and left them hanging nearly an hour, then lowered them down, and repeated the punishment, 'till they died or complied with the oath.

* * *

On the first of November, the fleet sailed up a narrow river, and anchored at night within two miles of a town called Little Whampoa. In front of it was a small fort, and several mandarine vessels

---

[4] Paddy refers to unhusked rice either growing in the field or already harvested.

lying in the harbour. The chief sent the interpreter to me, saying, I must order my men to make cartridges and clean their muskets, ready to go on shore in the morning. I assured the interpreter I should give the men no such orders, that they must please themselves. Soon after the chief came on board, threatening to put us all to a cruel death if we refused to obey his orders. For my own part I remained determined, and advised the men not to comply, as I thought by making ourselves useful we should be accounted too valuable.

A few hours afterwards he sent to me again, saying, that if myself and the quarter-master would assist them at the great guns, that if also the rest of the men went on shore and succeeded in taking the place, he would then take the money offered for our ransom, and give them twenty dollars for every Chinaman's head they cut off. To these proposals we cheerfully acceded, in hopes of facilitating our deliverance.

Early in the morning the forces intended for landing were assembled in row-boats, amounting in the whole to three or four thousand men. The largest vessels weighed, and hauled in shore, to cover the landing of the forces, and attack the fort and mandarine vessels. About nine o'clock the action commenced, and continued with great spirit for nearly an hour, when the walls of the fort gave way, and the men retreated in the greatest confusion.

* * *

After this the Ladrones returned, and plundered the town, every boat leaving it when laden. The Chinese on the hills perceiving most of the boats were off, rallied, and retook the town, after killing near two hundred Ladrones. One of my men was unfortunately lost in this dreadful massacre! The Ladrones landed a second time, drove the Chinese out of the town, then reduced it to ashes, and put all their prisoners to death, without regarding either age or sex!

I must not omit to mention a most horrid (though ludicrous) circumstance which happened at this place. The Ladrones were paid by their chief ten dollars for every Chinaman's head they produced. One of my men turning the corner of a street was met by a Ladrone running furiously after a Chinese; he had a drawn sword

FIGURE 14

Cutthroat Pirates of China (Charles Ellms, *The Pirates Own Book: Authentic Narratives of the Most Celebrated Sea Robbers*. Salem: Maritime Research Society, 1924.)

in his hand, and two Chinaman's heads which he had cut off, tied by their tails, and slung round his neck. I was witness myself to some of them producing five or six to obtain payment!!!

Richard Glasspoole, "A brief Narrative of my captivity and treatment amongst the Ladrones," in Charles Neumann, *History of the Pirates who Infested the China Sea from 1807 to 1810*. London: Oriental Translation Fund, 1831, pp. 107–119. Hamilton Library, University of Hawaii.

Doc. 22: *A Petition to Surrender, 1810*

Although there is controversy surrounding the authorship of this pirate petition to surrender of 1810, nevertheless it does represent the sentiments of many pirates at that time. Several scholars believe that either Zhang Bao or Guo Podai were the authors; others argue that the true author was Governor-General Bai Ling, who wrote it on behalf of the pirates to justify his pacification policy. As

Dian Murray has explained, "It begins by invoking past precedents for the par-
doning of serious offenders. After accounting for the rise of piracy, it makes its
appeal for sympathy through a pitiful depiction of life at sea. It is a rare and
detailed description of the pirates' lives and motivations."[1] This document,
regardless of authorship, was written at the height of the pirate disturbances in
Guangdong and at a time of severe food shortages and high prices caused by
severe famines in 1809 and 1810. There was a clear correlation, at least in the
mind of the author of this notice, between piracy, dearth, and the high cost of
food. Zheng Yi Sao and Zhang Bao, who were the most powerful pirate leaders
on the Guangdong coast since 1807, surrendered in April 1810, with over
17,000 followers, including men, women, and children.

Today we, your humble petitioners, are living in a prosperous age.
Originally we were meek and obedient subjects, but we became
[sea] bandits [for many reasons]. Because some of us were not
careful in choosing friends we fell among robbers. Others were unable to make a living or were kidnapped and forced into piracy
while trading on the lakes and rivers [i.e., oceans and seas]. Still
others, because of having committed a crime, joined this watery
world to escape punishment. At first there were only three or five of
us in a band, but later we increased to tens of thousands. Moreover,
because of the successive famines [in recent years], people had
nothing with which to maintain their livelihoods and as days and
months went by we had to take extraordinary actions. Had we
not resorted to robbery we could not have survived. Had we not
resisted the officials and soldiers our lives would have been in danger. Therefore, we violated the imperial laws and wrecked trade.
This was unavoidable.

Once we left our homes there was none among us who did not
yearn for our families. Drifting with wind and tide, each day we
were deeply troubled by our rootless lives. If we encountered government patrols, their cannon and arrows struck fear in our hearts.
If we met a display of force by the god He Po,[2] the great tempests
[that he caused] also frightened us. We fled to the east and to the

---

[1] Dian Murray, *Pirates of the South China Coast, 1790–1810* (Stanford: Stanford University
Press, 1987), p. 172.

[2] He Po was a popular sea deity, the god of the Yellow River.

west to avoid the pursuit of naval war junks. Having to sleep without shelter and eat in the wind, we suffered all the bitterness of the sea. At those times, we wanted to break away [from the pirates] and return to our homes, but our fellow villagers refused to accept us. We thought about surrendering as a group, but did not know what the powerful officials would do to us. Therefore, we had to remain on the islands just watching and waiting with no decision.

Alas! Our crimes, of course, should be punished by death. It is hard to evade the laws of the emperor. However, our situation is extremely pitiful and our survival must depend on benevolent men. We are happy that Your Honor [Governor-General Bai Ling], has returned to Guangdong to rule, for you regard others as yourself and love the people as your own children.[3]

We have respectfully read your proclamation several times. You advise us to surrender and you will take pity on our reasons for having become pirates. Your principle is to use both severity and leniency, and you understand that to spare lives is a heavenly virtue. In your justice you righteously employ both extermination and appeasement.[4] Even the bird flying in the dust seeks tranquility, so how can a fish be content in boiling water? For these reasons, we have gathered our followers to present to you this petition with our signatures. We humbly submit the remaining years of our lives to your mercy, hoping you will save us from flood and fire, pardon our former crimes, and permit us a new way of life from this day forward. We solemnly promise to sell our swords to buy oxen to plow the fields. In appreciation of your greatness we burn incense and praise you in song from the hilltops. If we dare to act with duplicity you may have us executed at once.

———————

Yuan Yonglun, *Jing haifen ji* [Record of the pacification of pirates], 1830. Translation by the Editor.

[3] Bai Ling, a Chinese Bannerman, had served earlier as Governor of Guangdong province in 1805, when he was recognized for his capable and fair administration. The Emperor later appointed him Governor-General in 1809, with the specific task of putting an end to the rampant piracy in the region.

[4] As soon as he arrived in Canton in April 1809, Bai Ling initiated an ancient strategy known as "extermination and appeasement" (*jiaofu*), a carrot-and-stick approach in which military campaigns were coupled with liberal offers of amnesties and rewards to pirates who surrendered.

Sea Raiders of Southeast Asia

Doc. 23: *An Oral History of Sea Dayak Raiding*

What Europeans called piracy was in the traditions and folklore of native Southeast Asians simply referred to as intertribal warfare. Benedict Sandin, who has recorded the oral history of the Iban or Sea Dayaks of his native Borneo, noted that about four generations before the arrival of James Brooke in Sarawak (1839) there occurred an important change in the social and political behavior of his people. Stories that had previously focused on pioneering now began to deal increasingly with raiding and intertribal warfare along the coast. A new sort of hero also emerged—the fearless warrior. According to Sandin, the new pattern of conflict was likely the result of population growth among the Ibans and their increasing contacts with other peoples living on other islands and along the coast, such as the Iranun of Sulu and Malay Muslims. The Ibans, who were well-known "head-hunters," went on raids for slaves and heads which they used in their religious sacrifices. Raiding was so central to Iban society and culture that most young warriors had the ambition to prove themselves in battle by capturing or slaying enemies and taking heads. Most of the battles described below took place during the first half of the nineteenth century between various groups of Sea Dayaks who lived at the mouths of different rivers in modern Sarawak.

At about this time, or perhaps slightly earlier, the Ibans first began to meet the Bajau and Illanun [Iranun] sea raiders. Operating from bases in the southern Philippines, sailing swift and heavy galleys which often mounted cannon, the Illanuns were in the habit of plundering far and wide throughout the Archipelago. As in the case of the Brunei tax collectors,[1] contact with the Ibans led to conflict and turmoil. One of the most famous Ibans who fought these pirates was Unggang (Lebor Menoa), the father of Luta, who defied the Brunei tax gatherers.

---

[1] The Ibans were ostensibly under the suzerainty of Malay Muslims from Brunei who attempted to impose a yearly "door tax" on the Ibans, a situation that led to numerous conflicts and tax revolts.

Unggang came from the Entanak, a small stream * * * which flows not far from the modern town of Betong. When he was a young warrior, Unggang dreamed that he travelled in a boat from the mouth of the Saribas [River] westward to Santubong Mountain, which is located on the coast near modern Kuching.

In his dream, after he landed he climbed the mountain. Halfway up, he met two very pretty maidens who had just finished bathing. One of them handed him a stone called *batu perunsut*, which she had used to rub her skin while bathing. She told him it was a most valuable charm, which he could use whenever he led his people to war. She also told him that none of the people who lived in the countries between the Santubong Delta and the mouth of the Saribas river could possibly beat him in battle. But she warned him that if he led his war parties beyond Santubong, southeastwards, then the stone she had given him would not guarantee his success.

The two maidens then told Unggang that they were Kumang and Lulong, who are the divine patronesses of successful warriors.

Shortly after he had this dream, Unggang built a large war boat, whose interior (*ruang*) was big enough for him to spread a large *idas* mat.[2] He used this boat to lead his warriors to guard the mouth of the Saribas river to prevent the Illanuns and other pirates from entering, and to attack other strangers who came to sail in that part of the South China Sea.

After he had done this successfully, he led his warriors further overseas to look for trading ships. He did not like to be accompanied by other Iban boats, as his own could easily carry over 100 warriors. At this time no one dared to attack any boat commanded by Unggang.

* * *

Another clash between the Sebuyaus and the people of Saribas took place in the time of Luta, the son of Unggang (Lebor Menoa) of Entanak. According to Saribas tradition, Luta's brother Ngadan

---

[2] An *idas* mat is a [coarse] mat made from rotan and bark. The Dayaks make their largest mats of the *idas* type [Sandin's note].

was murdered by the Sea Dayaks of Sebuyau itself. * * * In retaliation for this, Luta led the Saribas people to raid Sebuyau, where he killed many of the enemy.

It was not long after this that Luta and his brothers, Mulok and Ketit, set off on a trading expedition to Billiton Island, between Borneo and Java, in search of a shell called *tuchong*, valued for armlets. The party disappeared in the vicinity of Sungai Ubah, just beyond Tanjong Datu. Their fate remained a mystery; only fragments of their boat were found.

* * *

Despite these previous cases of hostility between the Saribas and Sebuyau Sea Dayaks, Iban tradition maintains that it was the Malay chief Indra Leia, who, not long before the arrival of James Brooke, stirred up serious warfare between the Ibans of the Saribas and Skrang on one hand, and those of the Undup and Lingga rivers and the various Sebuyau settlements on the other.

Indra Leia, the brother of Leia Pelawan and Leia Wangsa of Lingga, played a double game among the Ibans. Whenever he was in Saribas, he told the Saribas Dayaks that the Balau and Sebuyau Dayaks hated them, and vice versa. By keeping the Iban people in a constant state of warfare, he hoped to be able to control them for his own ends.

* * *

It was during this attack [against Banting] that Chulo (Tarang), a leading warrior of Linggir (Mali Lebu)[3] received his nickname (*ensumbar*). In the heat of the battle he jumped from the high open platform (*tanju*) of one of the Banting longhouses, carrying two valuable jars which he had looted, one over each arm, and holding a head which he had just taken in his mouth. 'I am Chulo,' he called out, "my name now is:

Tarang mandang Banting, Tarang mandang Lingga
Tarang mandang langit, Tarang mandang dunya"
("Light flashing over Banting, light flashing over Lingga.
Light shining in the heavens, light over the whole world.")

---

[3] The warrior chief Linggir (Mali Lebu) was Sandin's great-grandfather.

About three years later, the Orang Kaya Pemancha Dana (Bayang) led a large force against the Undup Ibans, who had killed his brother, Angkum. Long remembered as the "great *bala*" [or great war expedition, perhaps about 1845] this expedition completely defeated the Undups, many of whom were killed or taken captive. The survivors fled to Lingga and the Kapuas valley and settled in the Salimbau area.

* * *

Some time after the defeat of the Rimbas Sea Dayaks by the Balaus, * * * Linggir (Mali Lebu) of Paku led a large number of his warriors to attack the Melanaus of Ilas and Matu, on the coast. * * * In those days the Melanaus lived in extremely large longhouses built on very high posts. On this occasion, Linggir's force attacked one of the highest Melanau houses. It was strongly defended, and the attackers finally made a big fire under the house in order to smoke out the Melanaus, who were killed when they emerged. While they were making the fire, the Ibans protected themselves from spears hurled down at them by carrying canoes over their heads, in such a way that one canoe served as a shield for several men. More than a decade later, Linggir led similar attacks on Matu and Palo, both Melanau settlements, immediately before the battle of Betang Maru in 1849.

* * *

The Saribas and Skrang Ibans also began to make attacks on the Land Dayaks and Chinese who lived south and west along the coast in the vicinities of Pontianak and Sambas. At about the same time as Jiram's unsuccessful attack on the Kanowit Melanaus, the Orang Kaya Pemancha Dana (Bayang) started to raid Chinese settlers and others in Sambas territory. * * *

It was the habit of the Ibans when going on these raids, in which as many as 100 war boats might take part, to attack Land Dayak and Malay settlements along the intervening coasts between Saribas and Sambas, particularly if for some reason they decided not to go as far as the latter place.

About one year before the arrival of the White Rajah [James Brooke], Libau (Rentap) of Skrang led his warriors against settlements in the vicinity of Pontianak. But before he reached this area, he attacked the schooner of a Malay trader, capturing a cannon and some ammunition, as well as a kris [dagger] with a gold handle.

* * *

The Ibans had continued to raid the Serus since the days of Munan; indeed it was the ambition of nearly every young Iban warrior in the Saribas, as well as those who were already living in the Krian, to get one or more Seru heads. Chulo (Tarang), the leading warrior of Linggir (Mali Lebu), with Ugat of Paku were among those who are remembered for their success in conducting minor raids (*kayau anak*) against these pre-Iban people, now extinct.

Benedict Sandin, *The Sea Dayaks of Borneo before White Rajah Rule*. East Lansing: Michigan State University Press, 1968, pp. 63–77.

Doc. 24: *The Pirate Ah'moi*

In 1857, Chinese pirates operating off the coast of Vietnam abducted a Western seaman named Edward Brown. Among his captors was an overseas Chinese named Ah'moi, who hailed from Singapore and spoke English. Over the several months that Brown was held in captivity he befriended Ah'moi, who related to Brown the story of his life and how he fell in with the pirates. As the following story shows, Ah'moi, like other pirates around the world, led a somewhat checkered and dissolute life in which piracy was interspersed with occasional honest work. Like other pirates, too, Ah'moi was very mobile, moving quite freely about the South China Sea. Despite the strict prohibitions against piracy, it was common for pirates to operate out of British Hong Kong, where they were able to sell their booty and refit their vessels for cruises that took them into Southeast Asian waters.

My interpreter, whose name was Ah'moi, spoke English fluently, having been educated at Singapore. He became very intimate with me; and a short account of his history, *as he related it to me*, may not be altogether uninteresting to the reader here.

He was born at Singapore in the year 1832. His father, who was a general dealer [trader], had two Malay prahus [vessels]. At the age of twelve years, Ah'moi was sent on board one of these, bound to Penang. On her homeward-bound passage, she fell in with another prahu, smaller than herself, which his crew proposed to try to capture. He gave his consent to this, and, after a hard fight, they succeeded in taking her. He went on board of her; and, whilst his crew were busy searching below, he saw an old man lying on the deck, and dying from the wounds he had received during the action. Observing that he had something tied round his waist, he searched him, and found nine bars of gold tied up in an old silk scarf. He took the gold, and secreted it about his own person; and, fearing the man might revive, and inform his companions of it, he drew his knife, and put an end to him.

When he returned to Singapore, fearing that his father might become acquainted with this affair, by finding the treasure in his possession, he hid eight of the gold bars in the jungle. He sold one bar for two hundred and ninety rupees, went gambling, and in a few days lost the whole amount. Four more of his bars he spent in the same manner.

The father, becoming acquainted with his son's gambling propensity, desired to obtain some employment for him, where he would be kept more strictly than at his own home. He accordingly made application to have him admitted as a free pupil into the Missionary School, in which he succeeded. Ah'moi conducted himself with credit, and made rapid progress in his studies, till his sixteenth year. He left his remaining four bars of gold deposited in the same place as before, and occasionally visited them.

After he had been at this school three years and a half, he formed an acquaintance with a Malay woman of bad repute, who encouraged him to absent himself, and spend his time in her company. * * * At last he took up one of his gold bars, changed it for rupees, went to the house of his paramour, and commenced Opium smoking, which he has continued to this day.

* * *

He took up the remainder of his gold bars, gambled, and kept company with his paramour, until his last cash was spent, and he found himself diseased and destitute. In this condition, he returned to his paternal roof, where he remained for a year and a half, penitent, and endeavouring to redeem his past character. He formed resolutions never to gamble any more; but to lead an honest and industrious life in the future. * * *

Ah'moi had made great progress during his stay at the Missionary School, and could speak English tolerably well at this time. Through his father's interest, he was appointed as interpreter and supercargo[1] on board a British barque belonging to a Chinese house at Singapore, and bound to Shanghae [Shanghai]. There he was charged to sell a part of the cargo, from the proceeds of which he embezzled the sum of eight hundred dollars, and left the vessel.

* * *

Afterwards he joined Ah'pack's piratical fleet, then at Ningpo [i.e., Ningbo in China]. The vessel which he entered, whilst on a cruise, was chased by a British man-of-war brig, and the pirates, to save themselves, ran her on shore; but, as she drew ten feet of water, they had to swim a great distance to save themselves. Many of them were drowned, and some were shot, in the attempt. Ah'moi, however, with thirteen others, managed to reach the shore in safety, and were all that remained alive out of ninety-seven persons.

Having begged his way across the country, to Foo-chow-foo [i.e., Fuzhou, the capital of Fujian province], he obtained a passage to Hong-kong in a Portuguese lorcha.[2] When he arrived there, he was not long out of employment, but joined another piratical tymung [vessel], which cruised a short distance outside of Hong-kong, lying in wait for junks bound to Canton.

Several prizes were captured and taken into Hie-chee-chin Bay; those who could pay a ransom were allowed to proceed on their voyage again; but when the supercargo or owner could not pay what was demanded, the crew were put to torture, and the most barbarous means used to extort it; and if they failed, to use Ah'moi's

---

[1] The supercargo was the person on a merchant vessel who managed the commercial concerns of the voyage.

[2] Lorchas were hybrid Chinese and Southeast Asian vessels having two or three masts with a European-style hull but rigged like a Chinese junk.

own words—"we takee common sailor man first, and cuttee one head one day; then see'pose no can makee pay, must takee junk, makee burn; then no can pay, must takee allo piecee man, and kill him; so no got any man, can makee talk, what pidgin we makee do." At the expiration of two months, their tymung was laden with a general cargo, the fruits of plunder. When he returned to Hong-kong he was surprised to see a European come on board, and bargain for the cargo, which had to be sold below the market price, on account of the bags of sugar, baskets of dried fruit, &c., &c., having the names of the hongs [i.e., Chinese guilds] to whom they properly belonged, and to whom they had been consigned, written on them in large Chinese characters. But the European appeared to be well acquainted with those matters. He spoke the Canton dialect of Chinese as well as any person on board the tymung, and went by the name of Sam-qui.

"I saw our supercargo," said Ah'moi, "pay him a fifth share of the ransoms that had been taken during our cruise, amounting to above two thousand dollars. I had the curiosity to ask one of our crew (who had belonged to the tymung a considerable time) whether this European had any share in the vessel, and how it was that he received a portion of the ransoms. The man told me, that Sam-qui had *no* share in the vessel, but that he was the head man in Hong-kong, and that if he did not receive a cun-shaw (or present) after we made a good cruise, he would have us taken and punished as pirates; but so long as he profited by our plunder, we could go and come in safety, and he would supply us with English guns and powder in exchange for a portion of our cargo, and assist us to sell the remainder *safely*."

Ah'moi said, he had always been assured that Europeans were much averse to piracy, and that British men-of-war tried to suppress it; but since he witnessed this conduct in a European, who, he understood, had influence in Hong-kong, he has not half the dread he formerly had of being a pirate; for British men-of-war are all that pirates fear on the coast of China.

He remained fourteen months on board of this piratical tymung. The farthest place to which her cruise extended from Hong-kong was Cup-chi Point, distant about one hundred miles; her general places of resort were Bias and Ping-hoi Bays. She was seldom out longer than two months, before returning to Hong-kong, heavily laden with plundered merchandise. Sam-qui always received a fifth share of all specie or dollars that had been taken.

Ah'moi by this time had accumulated a small sum of money; and wishing to reform, and lead a more honest life, "fearing that his sins would overtake him," and that he would pay the penalty by an untimely death, he left his companions, and, purchasing a fishing boat, he set up as a pilot to European vessels entering the harbour of Hong-kong, of which he had acquired a thorough knowledge during his connection with the pirates. He found a great many of his countrymen in opposition to him in this business; but being able to speak English and Malay well, he succeeded famously for four months; when an untoward circumstance occurred to him.

One of his competitors had been acquainted with him when he was in his previous occupation, and had bought two chests of tea from him, bearing the mark of the hong to whom they originally belonged; and, as he had them still in his possession, he threatened that if Ah'moi continued piloting in Hong-kong in opposition to him, he would prosecute him for piracy, and bring forward the two chests of tea in proof. This was certainly very cruel on the part of his opponent in business, and was partly, if not wholly, the cause of his again becoming a pirate.

* * *

Ah'moi sold his boat for half the price he paid for it, gave up piloting, and hid himself from the sight of his jealous opponent. He had not left this business a month, before he met with Ching Ah'ling in Hong-kong, who was fitting out two small tymungs for a piratical expedition to the coast of Cochin-China [Vietnam]. Ah'moi joined him, and is now my interpreter and companion, serving in a fleet which has been increased to eight vessels, six of which were prizes, captured within the space of five months.

Edward Brown, *Cochin-China and My Experience of It. A Seaman's Narrative of his Adventures and Sufferings during a Captivity among Chinese Pirates, on the Coast of Cochin-China, and afterwards during a Journey on Foot across that Country, in the Years 1857–8*. London: Charles Westerton, 1861, pp. 52–59.

Doc. 25: *Drake's Island of Thieves, 1579*

Between 1577 and 1580, Francis Drake became the first English navigator to sail around the globe. After leaving the west coast of Spanish America, which he repeatedly pillaged, Drake crossed the Pacific Ocean in hopes of reaching the fabled Spice Islands. When he first made landfall, in September 1579, in the Caroline Islands (either at Yap or Palau) his reception was less than friendly. After the islanders tried to loot his vessel, a furious Drake christened the place the Island of Thieves. The selection below comes from a book, The World Encompassed, *written by his nephew and first published in London in 1628.*

* * * We departed againe [from the coast of California] the day next following, viz., *July* 25 [1579]. And our Generall now considering that the extremity of the cold not only continued, but increased, the Sunne being gone farther from us, and that the wind blowing still (as it did at first) from the Northwest, cut off all hope of finding a passage through these Northerne parts,[1] thought it necessarie to loose no time; and therefore with generall consent of all, bent his course directly to runne with the Ilands of the Moluccas [Spice Islands]. And so having nothing in our view but aire and sea, without sight of any land for the space of full 68 dayes together, wee continued our course through the maine Ocean [i.e., Pacific], till *September* 30 following, on which day we fell in kenne of certaine Ilands, lying about eight degrees to the Northward of the line.

From these Ilands, presently upon the discovery of us, came a great number of canowes [canoes], having in each of them in some foure, in some sixe, in some fourteene or fifteene men, bringing with them Coquos, fish, potatoes, and certaine fruites to small purpose. Their canowes were made after the fashion that the canowes of all the rest of the Ilands of Moluccas for the most part are, that is, of one tree, hollowed within with great art and cunning, being made so smooth, both within and without, that they bore a glosse, as if it were a harnesse most finely burnished. A prowe and sterne they had of one fashion, yeelding inward in manner of a semi-circle, of a great height, and hanged full of certaine white and

---

[1] Drake had sought to find a northern passage across the North American continent but had to abandon his plan due to the inclement weather he encountered.

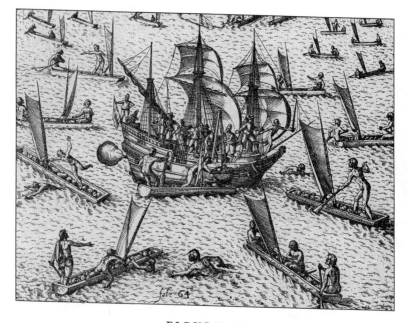

FIGURE 15
Pacific Islanders Attacking a European Ship (Theodor de Bry, *Collection des Grands and Petits Voyages.* London: Molins, 1921.)

glistering shels for bravery: on each side of their canowes, lay out two peeces of timber, about a yard and a haife long, more or lesse, according to the capacitie of their boate. At the ende whereof was fastned crossewise a great cane, the use whereof was to keepe their canowes from overthrowing, and that they might be equally borne up on each side.

The people themselves have the neather parts of their eares cut round or circlewise, hanging downe very low upon their cheekes, wherein they hang things of a reasonable weight: the nailes on the fingers of some of them, were at least an inch long, and their teeth as blacke as pitch, the colour whereof they use to renew by often eating of an herbe, with a kind of powder, which in a cane they carrie about them to the same purpose. The first sort and company of those canowes beeing come to our ship (which then, by reason of a scant wind, made little way), very subtilly and against their natures, began in peace to traffique with us, giving us one thing for another very orderly, intending (as we perceived) hereby to worke a greater mischiefe to us: intreating us by signes most earnestly to draw nearer towards the shore, that they might (if possible) make the easier prey both of the ship and us. But these passing away, and others continually resorting, wee were quickly able to guess at them what they were: for if they received anything once into their hands, they would neither give recompence nor restitution of it, but thought whatever they could finger to bee their owne, expecting alwayes with browes of brasse to receive more, but would part with nothing. Yea, being rejected for their bad dealing, as those with whom we would have no more to do, using us so evilly, they could not be satisfied till they had given that attempt to revenge themselves, because we would not give them whatsoever they would have for nothing: and having stones good store in their canowes, let flie a maine of them against us. It was farre from our Generals meaning to requite their malice by like injurie. Yet that they might knowe that he had power to do them harme (if he had listed) he caused a great peece to be shot off, not to hurt them, but to affright them.[2] Which wrought the desired effect amongst them, for at the noise thereof they every one leaped out of his canow into the water, and diving under the keele of their boates, staied them from going any way till our ship was gone a good way from them. Then they all lightly recovered into their canowes, and got them with speed toward the shoare.

Notwithstanding, other new companies (but all of the same mind) continually made resort unto us. And seeing that there was no good to be got by violence, they put on a shew of seeming honestie; and offering in shew to deale with us by way of exchange, under that pretence they cunningly fell a filching of what they could, and one of them puld a dagger and knives from one of our mens girdles, and being required to restore it againe, he rather used what meanes he could to catch at more. Neither could we at all be to ridde of this ungracious company, till we made some of them feel some smart as well as terror: and so we left that place, by all

[2] Another account reported that some twenty islanders were killed.

passengers to bee knowne hereafter by the name of the *Island of Theeves.*

M. N. Penzer, ed., *The World Encompassed and Analogous Contemporary Documents Concerning Sir Francis Drake's Circumnavigation of the World.* London: Argonaut Press, 1926, pp. 64–65.

Doc. 26: *Sulu Slave Raiding, early nineteenth century*

The following five cases come from the "Sulu Zone" in the southern Philippines and relate to the slaving activities of raiders in that region. Raiding was a normal aspect of life and, in many instances, a major source of livelihood. As the cases below show, some raiders voluntarily joined expeditions, but others had been coerced to join the pirates. Chiefs, nobles, and also the Sultan of Sulu were implicated in organizing raids—raiding was a state-sponsored activity. After capture, slaves were normally sold and resold many times. It was not uncommon for a slave to have had two or more masters in a lifetime, to have lived among several ethnic groups among the archipelagoes, and to have engaged in a variety of jobs for their masters.

1. Statement of a Balangingi raider named Silammkoom:
I am a native of one of the Sooloo [Sulu] Isles called Ballongningkin [Balanguingui] and I usually reside there. I sometimes trade in a small way such as selling Padi at Basilon and Mindanao. The Sultan lives at Sooloo proper. The principal Chief at Ballongningkin is Panglima Alip,[1] it is well inhabited and there are large fleets of boats which are employed in collecting sea weed, tortoise-shell, [and] trepang [sea cucumbers], . . . on account of the Sultan who gives the people in return, cloth or any other article he may think proper. Our fleet consisting of six prahus came from Ballongningkin and left that place about 3 months since. The fleet was commanded and under the sole direction of Orang Kaja Kullul, who is a relation of Panglima Alip. Orang Kaja Kullul informed us that the Sultan had desired him to plunder and capture all nations save Europeans. I have never seen the Sultan of Sulu, this is my first

---

[1] A panglima is a high-ranking noble.

voyage to the east coast of the Malayan Peninsula, but for many years I have cruized in the vicinity of Manillas, Macassar [Makassar] and other places on which occasion Orang Kaja Kullul took any boats he happened to meet.

2. Statement made by a "pirate" known as Daniel:
By birth I am an Illanun [Iranun] and for years have resided at Ballongningkin—for six years I have been pirating near Macassar, Myungka, Yan Le Lah, Seah-Seah, Tambulan, and other places. Panglima Alip is the chief of Ballongningkin, he is under the Sultan of Sulu. I cannot pretend to say whether the Sultan and Panglima Alip give any directions touching the fitting out of piratical fleets, but the fact is save "Mangoorays" (pirating) we have scarcely any other means of getting a livelihood. Six boats left Ballongningkin under the command of Orang Kaja Kullul . . . Talagoa was panglima of our boat . . . we had a crew of 29 men, six of whom were killed and several wounded.

3. Statement of captive named Man roon (alias Mah sandar):
I am a native of Ujang Pandan (? Pandars) Makassar—I was captured about two years since by a forminable Illanoon [Iranun] fleet consisting of 23 prahus—When I was taken I was proceeding to Mandas in company with 2 of my countrymen named Sindrah and Pannsil. After cruizing about for some time the piratical fleet went to Ballongningkin where I was treated as a slave and compelled to perform all kinds of work. Panglima Alip is the chief of Ballongningkin, and Orang Kaja Kullul is considered the second person in authority. The Sultan lives at Sooloo proper—We left Ballongningkin about 3 months since. The fleet consisted of six prahus— the whole under the command of Orang Kaja Kullul. I did not voluntarily join the pirates. I was compelled to go, two other of my countrymen (Sookut and Pula Nea) are in a similar position as myself. Ballongningkin is well peopled and I think there are about 200 prahus of the same size as the one destroyed by the steamer.

4. Statement of Tala Goa, a Balangingi raider:
I live at Ballongningkin with my family. I occasionally magoorap (pirating) [and] at other times [I am] making salt, planting Paddy, [or] collecting tortoise shell. I am a follower of Orang Kaja Kullul

and I am compelled to do and act as he may direct. Panglima Alip is the chief of Ballongningkin, he of course, was aware of the subject of the cruize and Orang Kaja Kullul received instructions not to molest trading boats to and from the ports of Singapore and Tringanoo. I can say nothing positively relative to the Sultan of Sooloo. I am not a panglima, I was placed in charge of one of the boats by Orang Kaja Kullul who had exclusive control of six prahus—the persons in charge of the several prahus were besides myself, See Deman, See Tambie, See Tundine, and See Puttah. Ballongningkin was destroyed by a force from Manilla when I was quite a youth.

5. Statement of an unnamed Filipino slave:
I was fishing for tripang [sea cucumber] with nine others in a small canoe near Masbate Island when we were pursued by four Balangingi baroto.[2] . . . One of my companions was killed when he resisted seizure . . . I was taken along with 150 other captives to Pilas island and allotted [as a slave]. I fell to Candayo, one of the nakodah [a ship's master]. After two months Candayo sold me at Jolo to the Muslim Siangu with whom I remained for eight years. Last year [1844] I accompanied my master to Palawan on a trading expedition, and while I was fishing two Balangingi pancos[3] passed and seized me. I was taken immediately to Pilas and sold.

James Warren, *The Sulu Zone, 1768–1898*. Singapore: Singapore University Press, 1981, pp. 240, 297–298.

Doc. 27: *Pirates of Lingga and Riau, 1818*

In this report M. H. W. Muntinghe, a Dutch colonial official, described several groups of indigenous raiders that were active in the waters around Singapore and the Malay Archipelago in 1818. The report makes clear that ethnic identity was closely related to sea raiding. Among the raiders, certain Malay groups, following

---

[2] A baroto was a sampan or dugout canoe with or without outriggers that was used as an auxiliary craft for inshore raiding.

[3] Spanish term for large Moro raiding craft of 50 to 90 feet in length.

the seasonal rhythms of the monsoons, alternated between fishing, gathering marine products, and raiding. The marine products that they collected for the Sultan of Lingga were important trade items in the Straits Settlements and in China. Another group of sea raiders, the Lanuns [Iranuns] of Sulu were the greatest threat to shipping in the whole region.

In 1818, we find in a report of Muntinghe, commissioner at Palembang and at Banka, numerous details regarding the piracies carried on by the inhabitants of Linga [Lingga], Rhio [Riau], and Biliton, all parts of the Johore Archipelago, the east coast of Sumatra, Carumatu [Karimata] and the west coast of Borneo. The piratical forces of Linga were under the command of subaltern chiefs of the Sultan of Linga, one fleet commanded by two brothers styled Orang Kaya Linga, consisting of 18 vessels and 400 men, and which had three points of rendezvous, Sakanah, Barok and Banachoong and the other under the command of Ungko Tamonggong, consisting of 48 vessels and about 1,200 men, which had seven places of rendezvous, Galang, Timian, Pulo Bocaya, Salat Singapura, (the Strait of Singapore) Sughi, Pakako and Bollang. These chiefs did not go upon the cruise themselves but fitted out the expeditions, furnishing the necessary provisions, stores and arms, and received repayment after a successful cruise with a profit of 100 per cent. The European arms became the prize of the Sultan, who could also select such other part of the spoil as he chose at a low price. These pirates every year undertook a regular voyage, of which the route was well known, and so calculated that they should always have the advantage of fair winds and currents. They set out towards the close of the western monsoon, or even during the months of December or January, and directing their course by the Straits of Sunda, towards the southern coast of Java, bore up at the commencement of the east monsoon. They then passed through one of the Straits to the east of Java, and ran along the eastern and northern coast of Java, which they infested till the commencement of May, when regaining the offing of their first route, they took the road to their coverts pillaging in passing the shores of Banca and Palembang. If they made an important prize they returned at once, but if as often happened, their voyage was unfruitful, they continued to infest these coasts until the close of the east monsoon, when they invariably regained their lairs, with or without booty. This they sold to the Chinese and other traders who came to Linga at a handsome profit. When prevented from proceeding on their piratical cruises, the pirates betook themselves to fishing for agar agar [sea weed] and tripang [sea cucumber], a means of livelihood still followed by the inhabitants of Linga, and who yet occasionally diversify their piscatorial pursuits by a little piratical outbreak. Before the European gunboat is on the spot they have again subsided into the appearance of peaceable fishermen, so that detection is very difficult. The pirates of Rete [Reteh] upon the coast of Sumatra, between the rivers of Jambi and Indragiri, were a race entirely distinct from the people amongst whom they were settled. They were all descended from the Lanuns [Iranuns]. They had first come to that part of the Archipelago by invitation of the Sultan of Linga to assist him, in a war with the Dutch E[ast] I[ndia] Company.[1] The strength of the Rete establishment was calculated at 1,000 men capable of bearing arms. The vessels were 10 or 12 in number of from 16 to 20 tons, and carrying from 50 to 80 men, and each having a large and two smaller pieces of ordnance. The descendents of these Lanuns are still to be found at Rete, but they are not distinguished for their piratical exploits like their fathers. Siak also sent out a small number of pirates. The island Biliton had two races of pirates belonging to it, who lived entirely on the water in small prahus covered with mats, forming a class entirely distinct from, the inhabitants of Biliton. The prahus in which they made their piratical expeditions were different from those in which they lived with their families. One of these races, the Suku Juru, had fifty small family prahus, and four piratical prahus. The other race, the Orang Sekat, had two hundred and thirty small prahus in which they resided and eighteen piratical prahua. These latter did not exceed

---

[1] Annoyed by the increasing maritime raids in the region, in 1784 the Dutch launched a successful attack on Riau and subjugated the kingdom. But three years later, the Sultan of Johor, with the help of Iranun warriors, expelled the Dutch from the island. Despite the victory, in the end the sultan soon left Riau for Lingga with a following of Bugis, Malays, and 200 wealthy Chinese merchants. With the decline of Riau, Lingga quickly became a major commercial and raiding hub.

four or six tons in burthen. The island of Carimater had two piratical prahus. The Sultan of Matani on the coast of Borneo had
three large piratical prahus of from 10 to 12 tons each, which
yearly, after a voyage towards the coast of Celebes in the western
monsoon, made three expeditions to the coast of Java.

Journal of the Indian Archipelago and Eastern Asia, 1850, vol. 4.

Doc. 28: *Handbill of William Edwards, 1845*

*In the 1830s and 1840s, handbills appealing for donations, which had been
printed by crippled and maimed victims of the Iranun, Balangingi, and other
maritime raiding groups in Southeast Asia, regularly circulated on the water-
fronts of Liverpool, Bristol, and Boston. The texts vividly describe the tragic fate
of some Asia-bound western seafarers who fell into the hands of these so-called
"Malay" pirates. In the example that follows, William Edwards had sailed
from Liverpool at the end of May 1844 on board the Jane Ann and returned
to Boston in late 1845 a shattered, silent man. The unfortunate seaman distributed his handbills in dockside taverns among drunken seafarers, prostitutes,
and crooks.*

TO A GENEROUS PUBLIC

I am a poor young man who have had the misfortune of having
my Tongue cut out of my mouth on my passage home from the
Coast of China, to Liverpool, in 1845, by the Malay Pirates, on the
Coast of Malacca. There were Fourteen of our Crew taken prisoners and kept on shore four months; some of whom had their eyes
put out, some their legs cut off, for myself I had my Tongue cut out.

We were taken about 120 miles to sea; we were then given a raft
and let go, and were three days and three nights on the raft, and ten
out of fourteen were lost. We were picked up by the ship James,
bound to Boston, in America, and after our arrival we were sent
home to Liverpool, in the ship Sarah James.

Two of my companions had trades before they went to sea, but
unfortunately for me having no Father or Mother living, I went to
sea quite young. I am now obliged to appeal to a Generous Public

for support, and any small donation you please to give will be thankfully received by

Your obedient servant,
WILLIAM EDWARDS.

P.S.—I sailed from Liverpool on the 28th day of May, 1844, on board the Jane Ann, belonging to Mr. Spade, William Jones, Captain. Signed by Mr. Rushton, Magistrate, Liverpool, Mr. Smith, and Mr. Williams, after I landed in Liverpool on the 10th December, 1845.

David Cordingly, ed., *Pirates: Terror on the High Seas—from the Caribbean to the South China Sea*, 1996, p. 204.

III

Interpretations

The Women Among the Boys

JO STANLEY

Other than the undisputable fact that there were female pirates sailing among the majority of male pirates, we know very little about the lives of those women. Who were they and why did they go to sea as pirates? How many female pirates were there? Taking a feminist perspective, Jo Stanley suggests possible answers to these questions. She warns, however, there was no such thing as a typical female pirate. She also rightly points out that women played important auxiliary roles as mothers, wives, lovers, prostitutes, cooks, spies, and suppliers for pirates. Stanley proposes that women went to sea not only to follow their husbands or lovers but also for adventure and as an act of defiance against a male-dominated world.

Amid the huge sweeping history of plundering at sea, involving thousands and thousands of sea brigands, are ten women. Their existence suggests that many more—overlooked and unrecorded—sailed the world's oceans. And hundreds of thousands more must have been deeply involved in the pirate world as lovers, wives, mothers, sex-industry workers, informants, fences, suppliers, nurses, cooks and seamstresses—because pirates did not exist in isolation, but in the world.

Ann Bonny and Mary Read[1] are the most famous women sea-rovers in Britain, not least because they worked in the early

[1] Ann Bonny and Mary Read served with Captain Rackam in the early eighteenth century. See Doc. 8 for Mary Read's biography [Editor].

eighteenth century, the period of piracy that is best recorded. At least one other woman pirate is known to have been active in that period: Maria Cobham.[2] As this was a high point in women's mobility, especially disguised as soldiers and sailors, it is inevitable that many more women than just Mary, Ann and Maria sailed the oceans. But there are far more stories of women pirates in plays and books than known women pirates[.]

* * *

There were perhaps several hundred women pirates during the thousands of years of piracy, with only a few pirate queens thanks to women's limited access to power. Cheng I Sao [Zheng Yi Sao] and Granuaile were pirate leaders because of family wealth and connections; Cheng I Sao commanded while clad metaphorically in her dead husband's cloak and breeches.[3] Given the familiar pattern even today of men mutinying against women's rule, there must be instances of widows failing to maintain their status as pirate captain (though I have found no records of this). There must also have been women who reached high status through merit rather than by virtue of their husband's or father's rank (records of their lives, too, are yet to be discovered).

At the other end of the social scale are the more lowly women who worked on pirate ships—women who might otherwise have been serving wenches or prostitutes, market traders or milkmaids. Some, such as Mary Read, were official crew members; others, such as Ann Bonny, were aboard informally for personal reasons. Mary Read was one of a number of working women masquerading as men in order to get a job at sea. Usually, a woman could not be a sailor in her own right (unless she was a woman of privilege: class and clout won out over gender every time). Records of female transvestites in the period from 1550 to 1830 confirm that women worked on ships in traditionally male roles such as deck hand, boatswain and carpenter.

[2] Maria Cobham was a prostitute-turned-pirate who lived at the end of the seventeenth century; she is possibly only a literary figure and not a real person [Editor].

[3] Granuaile or Grace O'Malley, who has been described as "the pirate queen of Ireland," lived in the late sixteenth century. On Cheng I Sao [Zheng Yi Sao], see Overview in this book [Editor].

Many pirates started off as seafarers and then changed ships. The transition from working on merchant vessels to privateers to pirate vessels could be seen as akin to the gradual move a woman might make from doing housework at home, to becoming a home help, to becoming an office cleaner—taking whatever opportunity she could to earn money in an increasingly alienated way, further from home. Mary Read is an example of a woman who slipped from working on privateers to the more outlawed world of the pirate vessel, but I suspect that if she reflected on her position the difficult issue was not so much the difference between being a woman on an ordinary ship and an outlawed women pirate as the transition from being a land-based woman to a woman seafarer. In stepping on board she breached the discouraging wall of hostility towards women at sea. For such working women, being on a pirate ship was a way to make a necessary living; they had no other wealth, unlike Granuaile for instance.

Accounts of general seafaring history indicate that there may have been women on ships who worked openly as females. My guess here is that ships unable to get a male crew together fast enough might have allowed women to sail, either openly or perhaps turning a blind eye to some implausible breeches. Men may have made this acceptable to themselves by setting women up as 'not proper pirates'—as adjuncts rather than workers in their own right: 'she is only helping him out; she is not really doing his job.'

By contrast to these openly female or 'out' women mariners, the 'out' women providers of services would have had the status of semi-independent traders, conducting their business (sex, most likely) within the main business of the ship, protected by an officer as a sponsor or type of pimp. It is a system that was later formalised as shop-keepers or barbers operated on a concessionary basis on passenger ships, paying a fee for being allowed to profit from the needs of the people the ship carried. A historian of nineteenth-century maritime life found that some captains of merchant vessels who wanted to retain their (scarce) male crew arranged to have sexually available women on hand—paid—to keep the crew happy. Such women may also have operated on pirate vessels in earlier times.

But the bulk of women pirates in the early eighteenth century were probably there because of their connection with male pirate leaders, working on their father's, husband's or lover's ship—as was Maria Cobham. This was certainly the usual reason for women's presence on non-pirate vessels. Mrs Croft in Jane Austen's 1818 novel *Persuasion* always sailed with her beloved Royal Naval husband and 'gloried in being a sailor's wife'. She claimed 'women may be as comfortable on board as in the best house in England. I know nothing superior to the acommodations of a man-of-war.' In pirate accounts such as Captain Charles Johnson's history, local women in the tropics were sometimes found on ship, seemingly as pirates' servants, especially when the ship was at anchor. This presence as men's sexual companions is a variation on the way pirate queens such as Cheng I Sao came into piracy—solely because of their connection with a husband or lover.

Popular mythology suggests that pirate captains' lovers traipsed round the decks in frilly frocks behaving boldly or bountifully as the second-in-command or even 'the real boss'. * * * But Maria Cobham, as Captain Cobham's wife, was reported to have made rules about how the crew should behave and to have intervened in her husband's decisions; other, less mythologised women may have been beloved or abused stooges. In Hollywood terms, their role was more likely to have been that of a gangster's dumb moll than a multi-skilled co-director of his international enterprise.

Counting Women In

When Ann Bonny and Mary Read were sailing, the estimated number of Anglo-American pirates ranged from 1,000 to 5,000. (At this time the total population of Liverpool was only 6,000 and the white population of the West Indies just 38,000. England and Wales had a population of 5.5 million—half the population of London today and nearly three times that of Jamaica now.) The number of pirates was less than one-tenth of the total number of common British seamen, which was 50,000 in 1688. * * * I propose that perhaps half of one per cent of these pirates could have been cross-dressed women, perhaps 50 to a few hundred.

An average of approximately 79 pirates worked on each ship in this period. Given all the incidences of exceptionalised women's presence that can be unearthed, it may be that some crews included as many as two females at times (after all, Mary Read and Ann Bonny were coincidentally on the same ship). In at least two other cases, there was a known woman working on privateers: Flora Bum was one of the 35-member crew of the *Revenge* and another woman was captain of a crew of a hundred. While recorded instances suggest that a surprising number of women may have been on ships, some pirates had a code of practice that forbade women to sail and may have forbidden their captain—or anyone else—to bring women aboard (unless they were shared out). So there may have been fewer 'out' women on pirate ships than on naval and merchant vessels.

Why Be a Woman Pirate?

Seafaring in all its different locations, cultures and periods has varied enormously: ships, food, crew, clothes, methods of fighting, frequency and type of encounter with targets, booty, opportunities ashore, reactions of people back home. But some general points can be made.

At best, a woman pirate's job satisfactions included adventure, wealth, an open-air life and the opportunity to see different places. The role offered a working-class woman extraordinary mobility, with the chance of doing well financially on some voyages and ending up if not with gold doubloons and trunks full of rubies, then at least with a length of saleable calico or tropical hardwood. The pleasures included the sweet taste of avenged wrongs (the Robin Hood motive) and the better food than naval ships; the self-regulation aboard as well as the fun—be it dancing or sonnet-writing. But I suspect that the problems of being a woman in a world of men who were deeply hostile to all that women stood for usually outweighed the joys.

Lesbians in the sixteenth, seventeenth and eighteenth centuries may have gained some limited freedom by passing as men on pirate and other ships. Historians of tranvestism Rudolf Dekker and Lotte van de Pol found, 'Sexual desire and love was thought of as something that could only be experienced with a male. We can therefore assume that most women who fell in love with other women could not place or identify those feelings. Therefore, it is logical that those women would think: if I covet a woman, I must be a man.'[4] If women cross-dressed and acted as men, it enabled them to love women at a time of longstanding European inability to conceive of lesbianism. A pirate vessel may not have been the best place for a 'Flatt'[5] to find her true love, but eighteenth-century Anglo-American pirate ships were known as places where people of all backgrounds were welcome—unlike naval ships. The relatively 'no questions asked' nature of pirate life could have meant that a pirate ship was a more likely place of employment for a cross-dressed woman than any other vessel.

Were these 'counterfeit men' changing their visible sexual identity as a way of challenging their destiny as women? Julie Wheelwright, in looking at cross-dressed woman soldiers, said that they 'appear largely unconcerned about changing the society that produced the inequity which they felt most keenly in their own lives . . . they traded roles rather than forged new ones.'[6] This suggests that women pirates who passed as men, as did Mary Read, were not early feminists seeking an existence that affirmed better values, but simply took men's places (perhaps uncritically) in dissatisfaction with their own. Although it was an attempt at a type of self-liberation, it was one with a limited perspective.

Some women may have been on pirate ships because they liked the company of male pirates, just as 1970s' ship girls relished seamen's companionship. * * * In the light of B. R. Burg's suggestions that there was extensive homosexual sex among seventeenth-century pirates working in the Caribbean, we might imagine pirate sloops appealing to fag hags. Though highly unlikely, this is a useful antidote to the usual view of gender relations aboard sloops as a simple scenario of butch men ravaging femme women. Much more complex relationships may yet be revealed[.] * * *

---

[4] Rudolf Dekker and Lotte van de Pol, *The Tradition of Female Transvestism in Early Modern Europe* (London: Macmillan, 1989), p. 57.

[5] "Flatt" as eighteenth-century slang for a lesbian is a reference to playing cards (flatts) and to the idea of the game of rubbing together two flat (i.e., non-projecting) genitals.

[6] Julie Wheelwright, *Amazons and Military Maids* (London: Pandora, 1989), p. 12.

Who Were Women Pirates?

There is no such typical, timeless thing as a 'woman pirate' any more than there is such a thing as a 'woman outlaw', 'woman warrior' or even a 'seafarer'. There are simply women in different periods and countries whose temporary livelihood was piracy. Those who commanded seafarers to rob and sailed with the mariners while they did so, as did Granuaile, were women used to leadership, negotiation and strategic daring on a grand scale. Others probably ranged from economic migrants to refugees from constricting homes; from women searching to ease misgivings about their sexuality to footloose itinerants unable to settle. They may have been hoydens hungry for violence or obedient workers who carried out instructions. The job could also have appealed to women who identified more with men than with women, for a variety of reasons. And it surely attracted women for the same reason as it attracted men—as a source of fast money and a way of escaping difficulties on land.

Women seafarers in the seventeenth, eighteenth and nineteenth centuries were mostly working-class women who would have been expected to stay on land and keep house. Just as women healers and wise women refused to accept their male-alloted roles, so women seafarers expressed their discontent with domestic labour by leaving the milieu deemed appropriate for them and moving into a more public sphere. Feminist sociological studies show that women who break out of old patterns require courage, impetus, an ability to be hard when appropriate, curiosity, a huge need for change and shrewdness to see and act upon opportunities. Women seafarers were probably choosing a way of living never before experienced by any woman in their family, forging a new mould and perhaps unconsciously demonstrating the need for a change in women's social position.

Some women may have had knowledge or experience that made them hungry for a larger world. Obviously pirates did not write home urging their relatives to take up the trade. But being in a coastal community would have given women access to seafarers and stories of seafaring. The idea that women could be sea-rovers was enshrined in popular ballads and dramas of the eighteenth century which celebrated the feats of cross-dressed women (even if some did come to terrible ends) and there is some evidence that these led more women on land to don breeches. But by depicting women sailors, soldiers and outlaws as bold, brave, unusual and ultimately happy to marry, the ideology such works built up denied that other parts of the female population were struggling for less fettered lives.

To be 'born with the sea in your blood' implies a knowledge or orientation passed on through families, usually to men. Women too may have experienced a longing for the sea, when the same blood flowed in their veins, the same stories flowed into their ears and the same nearby ocean assailed their nostrils. Desire must have been created by proximity to possibilities coupled with an interest in new experiences and perhaps a sense that there was nothing to lose. Piracy may have seemed a natural step to women already outlawed by working at sea or as dockside prostitutes. Or it might have appeared better and more profitable than anything else available. In some cases it appears to have been an activity people fell into as the result of a train of accidents, as Mary Read's life demonstrates.

Piracy was probably not an occupation young girls dreamed of in the way that young women in the 1960s saw being an air hostess as the height of excitement. Nor was it that piracy appealed to angry viragos who lusted to commit brutalities and improve their street credibility, as male SM fantasy might have it. It was probably not something women felt they had a vocation for, like working in a convent healing the sick. It was just an option that presented itself. Male pirates, and Mary Read herself, told courts they were only pirates reluctantly and would rather go straight in much the same way as studies of prostitutes show that some women take up the work out of necessity and will continue only until they earn enough to retire.

If there is a common factor among women pirates in different periods and cultures, it is probably that piracy seemed the best available option in their situation. It is likely that they were women with little sense that they could change their destiny; not because of any failure of imagination but because they were products of their period. The possibility of wearing trousers—of a new way of behaving as a woman—acted as a psychic green light, however little it was consciously recognised as such.

Wearing the Breeches

Accounts of women pirates in different periods—Alfhild, Ann Bonny and Mary Read, as well as Lai Choi San—say they wore trousers.[7] These accounts should not be taken at face value—it may be that storytellers had to make women sound like men or almost men to accommodate the idea that they could be pirates at all. But on the other hand, wearing trousers did make practical sense. The reason most women donned breeches was to travel safely, to avoid molestation and to get into situations where only men were supposed to be. Wearing trousers allowed women pirates the freedom to climb, work with ropes, go up and down ladders. Anything that dragged in puddles on open decks would have been a nuisance and could have taken days to dry. It was easier to afford, launder, patch or replace breeches than boned bodices and several layers of skirt. Women may also have worn these clothes for the reasons people wear any work uniform: they thought they had no choice; the clothes indicated admission to corporate identity; such clothing was all that was available after months at sea; breeches were proven to be practical and utilitarian. And trousers were also protection against wandering hands and sexual harassment.

* * * While I believe women wore trousers primarily on practical grounds, there may have been less conscious reasons as well. For instance, some lesbians may have worn breeches as part of living out a masculine identity. Breeches could also be taken as a statement that women were seizing power, laying claim to the privileges of the more powerful group: like power-dressing, they may have been both a conscious and unconscious way of appropriating the trappings of authority. Breeches—in illustrations if not in reality— also indicate that the women pirates are part of an oppositional gang removed from land values, in much the same way as young women gangs such as the Slick Chicks and Black Widows in the US

[7] Alfhild was a female Danish pirate who lived about the year 400, and Lai Choi San was a female pirate who lived in South China in the early twentieth century [Editor].

of the 1940s wore zoot suits to indicate their place in an aggressive, rebellious movement.

Conversely, by wearing trousers women pirates may have been capitulating to men and reassuring themselves of their acceptance by men. As Elizabeth Wilson points out in *Adorned in Dreams*, today:

> . . . while the trousers for women might symbolize a myth in Western societies that women have achieved emancipation, it can hardly be interpreted as unproblematic of their status. If it were interpreted in this literal way it would lead us to think . . . that in so far as women have made progress in the public sphere of paid work, this has been on male terms and within the parameter of masculine values.[8]

Women pirates in breeches would not necessarily have been an indication that progress was being made, but simply a sign of women's continued confinement.

Interpreting the Breeches

* * * Cross-dressing is a significant part of the mythology of women pirates, with its implication of a woman who is stepping out of her usual station, taking power. As *The Shorter Oxford Dictionary* notes, 'To wear the breeches: to be master, said of a wife.' The phrase is used derogatively against both the woman (too butch) and the man who allowed it (too soft). And as used by some men, there is also an implicit, sexualised, masochistic admiration.

Breeches—as coverings for absent phalli—have been fetishised by western culture as a way of dealing with women who take on unwomanly roles. Ninety per cent of illustrations of women pirates play on their masculine attire, a play which is especially apparent in the movie *Anne of the Indies* (made just after the Second World War when more western women wore trousers than at any previous time). Illustrators and writers of pirate tales, the majority of readers until the late nineteenth century and Hollywood film-makers have mostly been male. Presenting women pirates in swashbuckling

---

[8] Elizabeth Wilson, *Adorned in Dreams: Fashion and Modernity* (New Brunswick: Rutgers University Press, 2003), p. 165.

breeches is an expression of the narcissistic assumption that men are the prototype and women the adaptation, the pirate-ess, the mini-version of 'proper' male pirates.

Fashion analyst Anne Hollander has argued that in the twentieth century the female leg symbolises movement. While some illustrations of women pirates show immobile legs swathed in voluminous drapery, * * * many popular nineteenth- and twentieth-century images show their legs trousered and active—fighting, walking, lunging, standing threateningly—to a degree unusual among male portrayals of women. The fact that breeches are short, cut off at the knee, and that the lower leg is either naked or encased in a tight-fitting boot that reveals its shape indicates movement more dramatically than, say, bell-bottoms or leggings. Western men have long fetishised fragments of women's bodies such as legs or breasts. The nude leg hints that eighteenth- and nineteenth-century men saw women pirates as having an animal sexual availability, especially outrageous and exciting in the Victorian period when even piano legs had to be swathed for fear they would incite lustful thoughts.

Women who take up public space have been seen in many cultures as sexually available. Such a woman is not chastely in her own home with her own man; her eyes are not cast down and her mouth is not closed in a compliant smile. To wear the trousers in public is a daring transcendence of woman's traditional role as well as an indication that the woman in question is not maidenly but available for sex (whether or not she is hypocritically chastised for that). * * * However much the woman might be cross-dressing for sexual safety, the outside world sets her up as all the more sexually desirable and accessible. Elizabeth Wilson points out that:

> For centuries western women's legs had been concealed, trousers and pantaloons worn only by actresses, acrobats and women of dubious morality. . . until the 1900s only working women, and then usually only those engaged on the coarsest labour, and entertainers, wore trousers and showed their legs, and when they did so their morality was impugned.

Wilson adds that roaming field gangs of women agricultural workers, sometimes wearing trousers, were seen by the Medical Officer of the Privy Council in 1864 as 'looking wonderfully strong but tainted with a customary immorality and heedless of the fatal result which their love of this busy and independent life is bringing on their unfortunate offspring who are pining at home.'[9]

The mere fact of wearing breeches places a woman pirate in reality or fiction in the position of a sexualised outlaw. Breeches reinforce the idea that only 'strange' women can work at sea and that if you want to work on ship, the price you pay is loss of feminine identity. If wayward members of society are so visibly proved to be strange or abnormal it renders the centre more safe.

How Did Women Pirates Feel?

One of the exciting aspects of writing women's history is to imagine how women who have been called unusual, wayward or not quite human might have felt. How can we guess what women pirates were conscious or unconscious of being? How can we understand the women as individuals and as products of a particular world? One answer is to speculate on the basis of what we know of women in male work situations today, as described in occupational sociology books and newspaper reports.

On the positive side, women pirates may have felt bold, free and full of excitement at their ability to meet unfamiliar challenges, sentiments echoed by some women admitted into the armed services during the Second World War. Those less powerful than the pirate queens may have felt the same determination to fight against male hostility shown in fire stations, the composing rooms of the print trade and police departments today. Sometimes they might have been defeated: even high-ranking women today have been unable to face the prospect of more years of harassment and have left their jobs. A young New Zealand woman working on fishing trawlers described at a recent 'Woman and the Sea' conference her anger at being sabotaged for not co-operating sexually with male colleagues, at twice being dumped in foreign ports and at having to change jobs nine times because of the intolerable daily injustices. Other women

[9] *Ibid.*, p. 162.

seafarers have been able to persevere because they have had women around them to support them and share their moans. A woman pirate alienated by the restrictive conventions of shore life may have hoped for and found a more compatible existence on pirate ships; her sense of whether or not it was an improvement would be determined by how badly she had been treated elsewhere.

Surveys of women at work show that they want to be respected and not made into the butt of lewd remarks, gropings or rapes. But because pirates and seamen were used to warfare and to sometimes mutually exploitative relationships with women, violence and abuse were far from exceptional. Pirates' captives of both sexes were tortured. When captives were women, especially black women, men's violence was sexualised. Exquemelin tells many tales of gang rapes by buccaneers. Violence by pirates was influenced by xenophobia too, and black women—captives and colleagues—must have been even more threatened. A woman pirate might have felt constantly under threat of male violence and have had to indicate by every means possible, especially tough body language, that she was not to be abused. Competent work skills could have earned her respect and some safety as well as a way into future jobs.

Seafarers were frequently beset by boredom, especially when ships lay becalmed. And people often say that a day at sea is twice as long as a day on land, so a pirate may have appreciated high-adrenalin engagements when they arose. Studies on the psychology of confrontation show that such encounters can arouse fear, excitement and an exalting sense of power, though post-combat trauma can bring depression, terror and guilt. If women pirates were involved in extensive fighting, their later reactions may have been similar to the rage, despair and sense of futility experienced by soldiers returning from the Vietnam, Falklands and Gulf wars. The nightmares never stop and human relationships are impossibly scarred. And women pirates today may well feel like and stage themselves as under-privileged citizens driven to work in the alternative economy, like Philippines mail-order wives or Piccadilly Circus rent boys.

Of course, we will never know how women pirates feel and felt since this has never been described by the women themselves or by people in search of authenticity rather than sensationalism. But we can put ourselves into these sea-brigands' sailcloth breeches and imagine.

Jo Stanley, ed., *Bold in Her Britches: Women Pirates across the Ages*. San Francisco: Pandora, 1995, pp. 36–48.

Hydrarchy and Libertalia: The Utopian Dimensions of Atlantic Piracy in the Early Eighteenth Century

MARCUS REDIKER

Depicted as swashbuckling heroes or as the "common enemy of mankind," pirates have been both romanticized and vilified. Most pirates were common sailors who, because of poverty and harsh working conditions aboard merchant and naval vessels, took control of their own lives to create a distinctly different society. According to Rediker, pirates created a "world turned upside down"— one that was democratic in an undemocratic age. Early eighteenth-century Western pirates took the law into their own hands by electing their officers, writing their own codes of behavior, and sharing their booty equitably. Rediker argues that they challenged prevailing notions of class, race, gender, and nationality. But did the same sort of views apply to pirates everywhere and at all times?

A Pirate Utopia

Edward Braithwaite, a clever and knowledgeable seventeenth-century observer of things maritime, once remarked that sailors lived 'in a Hydrarchy'. By this he meant that sailors were a peculiar lot whose customs and social lives were formed by their long, isolated stints of work at sea. In this chapter I will use Braithwaite's term to designate the self-rule and social order devised and deployed by pirates during the early eighteenth century, though I also wish to suggest that Hydrarchy was not entirely peculiar, either to pirates or to sailors. Rather, I will argue that it was a volatile, serpentine tradition of opposition—now latent, now mobilized—within both maritime and working-class culture. Within the history of early modern Atlantic radicalism it reared its head again and again, emerging as a distinctly proletarian form of republicanism in the age of revolution.[1]

A version of Hydrarchy appeared in the first chapter of volume II of *A General History of the Pyrates* (1728), which tells the tale of Captain Misson and his fellow pirates who established a Utopian republic in Madagascar called 'Libertalia'. Their settlement looked backward to the ancient prophecy that paradise would be found on the east coast of Africa; it was itself a prophetic glance toward future societies to be based on the revolutionary ideals of liberty, equality and fraternity. Libertalians would be 'vigilant Guardians of the People's Rights and Liberties'; they would stand as 'Barriers against the Rich and Powerful'. By waging war on behalf of 'the Oppressed' against 'the Oppressors', they would see that 'Justice was equally distributed'.

When it came to self-rule, Misson's pirates 'look'd upon a Democratical Form, where the People themselves were the Makers and Judges of their own Laws, [as] the most agreeable'. They sought to institutionalize their commitment to 'a Life of Liberty', which they took for a natural right. They stood against monarchy, preferring to elect and rotate their leaders: 'Power . . . should not be for Life, not hereditary, but determinate at the end of three Years'. They limited the power of their principal leader, who was never to 'think himself other than their Comrade' and was to use his power 'for the publick Good only'. They chose their council, their highest authority, 'of the ablest among them, without Distinction of Nation or Colour'.

Misson's pirates were anti-capitalist, opposed to the dispossession that necessarily accompanied the historical ascent of wage labour and capitalism. They insisted that 'every Man was born free, and had as much Right to what would support him, as to the Air he respired'. They resented the 'encroachments' by which 'Villains'

---

[1] The themes of this essay are treated at greater length and in a broader context in Peter Linebaugh and Marcus Rediker, *The Many-Headed Hydra: Sailors, Slaves, Commoners, and the Hidden History of the Revolutionary Atlantic* (Boston: Beacon Press, 2000) [Editor].

and 'unmerciful Creditors' grew 'immensely rich' as others became 'wretchedly miserable'. They spoke of the 'Natural right' to 'a Share of the Earth as is necessary for our Support'. They saw their piracy as a war of self-preservation.

Men who had been 'ignorant of their Birth-Right, and the Sweets of Liberty' would recapture lost freedoms and guarantees of well-being in Libertalia, and they would do so by redefining fundamental relations of property and power. They had no need for money 'where every Thing was in common, and no Hedge bounded any particular Man's Property', and they decreed that 'the Treasure and Cattle they were Masters of should be equally divided'. Formerly seamen, wage labourers, and perhaps even victims of dispossession themselves, these pirates would finally have 'some Place to call their own', where 'the Air was wholesome, the Soil fruitful, the Sea abounding with Fish', where they would enjoy 'all the Necessaries of Life'. '[W]hen Age or Wounds had render'd them incapable of Hardship', Libertalia would be a place 'where they might enjoy the Fruits of their Labour, and go to their Graves in Peace'.

Concerns over 'Birth-rights', 'the Sweets of Liberty' and the 'Fruits of Labour' were broad enough to include the abolition of slavery. Misson observed that 'Trading for those of our own Species, cou'd never be agreeable to the Eyes of divine Justice: That no Man had power of Liberty of another'. He 'had not exempted his Neck from the Galling Yoak of Slavery, and asserted his own Liberty, to enslave others'. Misson and his men thus took slaves from captured slave ships and incorporated them into their own social order as 'Freemen'. They were literally a motley crew, half black and half white on some of their vessels, made up of African, Dutch, Portuguese, English and French (Catholic and Huguenot) seamen. Misson 'gave the Name of *Liberi* to his People, desiring in that might be drown'd the distinguish'd Names of *French, English, Dutch, Africans, &c*'. Libertalia made room for many cultures, races and nations.

Thus did Misson and his men create a radical-democratic utopia that condemned dispossession, capitalist property relations, slavery and nationalism, as it affirmed justice, democracy, liberty and popular rights. Of course it was all a fiction, or so we have been told by scholars who have for many years insisted that the author of *A General History of the Pyrates* was in fact Daniel Defoe, writing under the pen name Captain Charles Johnson. But was it a fiction? Since a man named Misson and a place named Libertalia apparently never existed, the literal answer must be yes. But in a deeper historical and political sense Misson and Libertalia were not simply fictions. Christopher Hill has recently detected in Misson's Utopia the lingering influence of the popular radicalism of the English Revolution.[2] A group of pirates had, after all, settled in Madagascar in a place they had 'given the name of Ranter Bay', named, it would seem, after the most radical of the Protestant sects of the English Revolution.

In this chapter I wish to carry Hill's argument further by suggesting that Libertalia was a fictive expression of the living traditions, practices and dreams of an Atlantic working class, many of which were observed, synthesized and translated into discourse by the author of *A General History of the Pyrates*. A mosaic assembled from the specific Utopian practices of the early eighteenth-century pirate ship, Libertalia had objective bases in historical fact. Hydrarchy came ashore as Libertalia.

The Maritime World Turned Upside Down

The pirate ship, like Libertalia, was a 'world turned upside down', made so by the articles of agreement that established the rules and customs of the pirates' social order. Pirates 'distributed justice', elected their officers, divided their loot equally, and established a different discipline. They limited the authority of the captain, resisted many of the practices of capitalist merchant shipping industry, and maintained a multicultural, multiracial, multinational social order. They demonstrated quite clearly—and subversively—that ships did not have to be run in the brutal and oppressive ways of the merchant service and the Royal Navy.

On the high seas, as in Libertalia, pirates elected their leaders democratically. They gave their captain unquestioned authority in

---

[2] Hill was the first scholar to note the "survival of Utopian and radical ideas" among pirates. See Christopher Hill, "Radical Pirates?" in *The Origins of Anglo-American Radicalism*, ed. Margaret Jacob and James Jacob (London: Allen & Unwin, 1984), pp. 17–32 [Editor].

chase and battle, but otherwise insisted that he be 'governed by a Majority'. As one observer noted, 'they permit him to be Captain, on Condition, that they may be Captain over him'. They gave him few privileges: no extra food, no private mess, no special accommodations. Moreover, the majority giveth and it taketh away, deposing captains for cowardice, cruelty, refusing 'to take and plunder English Vessels', or even for being 'too Gentleman-like'. Captains who dared to exceed their authority were sometimes executed. Most pirates, 'having suffered formerly from the ill-treatment of their officers, provided carefully against any such evil' once free to organize the ship after their own hearts. Further limitations on the captain's power appeared in the person of the quartermaster, who was elected to represent and protect 'the Interest of the Crew', and in the institution of the council, the democratic gathering that usually involved every man on the ship and always constituted its highest authority.

The 'equal division' of property in Libertalia had its basis in the pirates' shipboard distribution of plunder, which levelled the elaborate hierarchy of pay ranks common to maritime employments and dramatically reduced the distance between officers and common men. Captain and quartermaster received one and a half to two shares; minor officers and craftsmen, one and a quarter or one and a half; all others got one share each. Such egalitarianism flowed from crucial, material facts. By expropriating a merchant ship (after a mutiny or a capture), pirates seized the means of maritime production and declared it to be the common property of those who did its work. They also abolished the wage relation central to the process of capitalist accumulation. So rather than work for wages using the tools and larger machine (the ship) owned by a merchant capitalist, pirates now commanded the ship as their own property, and shared equally in the risks of their common adventure.

Pirates acted as 'vigilant Guardians of the Peoples Rights and Liberties' and as 'Barriers against the Rich and Powerful' when they took revenge against merchant captains who tyrannized the common seaman and against royal officials who upheld their bloody prerogative to do so. The Libertalian's comment about overseeing 'the Distribution of Justice' referred to a specific practice among pirates by the same name. After capturing a prize vessel, pirates 'distributed justice' by inquiring about 'the Commander's Behaviour to their Men'. They 'whipp'd and pickled' those 'against whom Complaint was made'. * * * Pirate captain Howell Davis claimed that 'their reasons for going a pirating were to revenge themselves on base Merchants and cruel commanders of Ships'.[3] Still, pirates did not punish captains indiscriminately. They often rewarded the 'honest Fellow that never abused any Sailors' and even offered to let one decent captain 'return with a large sum of Money to London, and bid the Merchants defiance'. Pirates thus stood against the brutal injustices of the merchant shipping industry, one crew claiming to be 'Robbin Hoods Men'. * * *

Many observers of pirate life noted the carnivalesque quality of their occasions—the eating, drinking, fiddling, dancing, and merriment—and some considered such 'infinite Disorders' inimical to good discipline at sea. Men who had suffered short or rotten provisions in other maritime employments now ate and drank 'in a wanton and riotous Way', which was indeed their 'Custom'. They conducted so much business 'over a Large Bowl of Punch' that sobriety might even bring 'a Man under a Suspicion of being in a Plot against the Commonwealth'. The very first item in Bartholomew Roberts's articles guaranteed every man not money but rather 'a Vote in Affairs of Moment' and 'equal Title' to 'fresh provisions' and 'strong Liquors'. For some who joined, drink 'had been a greater motive . . . than Gold'. Most would have agreed with the motto: '*No Adventures to be made without Belly-Timber*'.

The real pirates of the Atlantic made efforts to provide for their health and security, their own 'self-preservation', as did the settlers at Libertalia. The popular image of the freebooter as a man with a patched eye, a peg leg and a hook for a hand is not wholly accurate, but still it speaks an essential truth: sailoring was a dangerous line of work. Pirates therefore put a portion of all booty into a 'common fund' to provide for those who sustained injuries of lasting effect, whether the loss of eyesight or any appendage. They tried to provide for those rendered 'incapable of Hardship' by 'Age or Wounds'.

---

[3] See Doc. 7 in this book [Editor].

One of the most distinctive features of Misson's Utopia was its attack on slavery. Did it have basis in historical fact? The answer to this question—and indeed the entire record of relations between pirates and people of African descent—is ambiguous, even contradictory. A substantial minority of pirates had worked in the slave trade and had therefore been part of the machinery of enslavement and transportation. And when pirates took prize vessels, as they did near African and New World ports, slaves were sometimes part of the captured 'cargo', and were in turn treated as such, traded or sold as if commodities like any other. Pirates were occasionally said to have committed atrocities against the slaves they took.

But it must also be noted that people of African descent made up crucial parts of pirate crews. A few of these men ended up 'dancing to the four winds', like the mulatto who sailed with Black Bart Roberts and was hanged for it in Virginia in 1720. Another 'resolute Fellow, a Negroe' named Caesar stood ready to blow up Blackbeard's ship rather than submit to the Royal Navy in 1718; he too was hanged. Black pirates also made up part of the pirates' vanguard, the most trusted and fearsome members of the crew who boarded a prospective prize. * * *

These were not exceptional cases, for 'Negroes and Molattoes' were present on almost every pirate ship, and only rarely did the many merchants and captains who commented on their presence call them 'slaves'. Black pirates sailed with Captains Bellamy, Taylor, Williams, Harris, Winter, Shipton, Lyne, Skyrm, Roberts, Spriggs, Bonnet, Phillips, Baptist, Cooper, and others. In 1718, 60 of Blackbeard's crew of 100 were black, while Captain William Lewis boasted '40 able Negroe Sailors' among his crew of 80. In 1719 Oliver La Bouche had a ship that was, like Misson's, 'half French, half Negroes'. Black pirates were common enough—and nightmare enough—to move one newspaper to report that an all-mulatto band of sea-robbers was marauding the Caribbean, eating the hearts of captured white men!

Some black pirates were free men, perhaps like the experienced 'free Negro' seaman from Deptford, England, who in 1721 led a 'a Mutiny that we had too many Officers, and that the work was too hard, and what not'. Others were runaway slaves. In 1716 the slaves of Antigua had grown 'very impudent and insulting', causing their masters to fear an insurrection. Hugh Rankin writes that a substantial number of the unruly 'went off to join those pirates who did not seem too concerned about color differences'.[4]

* * *

Too little is known about black pirates, yet we must conclude that pirates as a whole in the early eighteenth century did not self-consciously attack slavery as was done in Misson's Utopia, neither did pirates adhere to the strict racial logic that polarized a great many societies around the Atlantic. Some slaves and free blacks seem to have found relative freedom aboard the pirate ship, which was no easy thing for many to find, especially in the Caribbean. The very existence of black pirates, contradictory though their lives probably were, may well have moved the author of *A General History of the Pyrates* to imagine the deeper critique of slavery at work in Libertalia.

Africans and African-Americans were but one part of a motley crew, in Libertalia and aboard most pirate ships. Governor Nicholas Lawes of Jamaica echoed the thoughts of royal officials everywhere when he called pirates a 'banditti of all nations'. Black Sam Bellamy's crew was 'a mix't multitude of all Country's', as were the principal mutineers aboard the *George Galley* in 1724: an Englishman, a Welshman, an Irishman, two Scots, two Swedes and a Dane, all of whom became pirates. Benjamin Evans's crew consisted of men of English, French, Irish, Spanish and African descent. When hailed by other vessels, pirates emphasized their rejection of nationality by replying that they came 'From the Seas'. And as a mutineer had muttered in 1699, 'it signified nothing what part of the World a man liv'd in, so he Liv'd well'. Such was the separatist logic that led to the founding of Libertalia.

The War against Libertalia

The Utopian features of the pirate ship were crucial to both the recruitment and reproduction of the group, and eventually to its

---

[4] Hugh F. Rankin, *The Golden Age of Piracy* (New York: Holt, Rinehart and Winston, 1969), p. 82 [Editor].

suppression, for both pirates and the English ruling class recognized the power of Hydrarchy and its alternative social order. Some worried that pirates might 'set up a sort of Commonwealth' in areas where 'no Power' would be 'able to dispute it with them'. Colonial and metropolitan merchants and officials feared the incipient separatism of Libertalia in Madagascar, Sierra Leone, Bermuda, the Bay of Campeche, and other regions. If Libertalia was a working-class dream, it was equally (and necessarily) a ruling-class nightmare.

* * *

It is not hard to understand why these men joined. The prospect of plunder and 'ready money', the food and the drink, the cama-raderie, the democracy, equality, and justice, the promise of care for the injured—all of these must have been appealing. The attractions were perhaps best summarized by Bartholomew Roberts, who remarked that in the merchant service 'there is thin Commons, low Wages, and hard Labour; in this, Plenty and Satiety, Pleasure and Ease, Liberty and Power; and who would not ballance Creditor on this Side, when all the Hazard that is run for it, at worst, is only a sower Look or two at choaking. No, *a merry Life and a short one*, shall be my motto.'

The English ruling class was less than keen about the merriment, but more than happy to oblige Roberts and his men in making their lives short ones. The 5,000 or so pirates who haunted the sea lanes of the Atlantic had made a great deal of 'Noise in the World'—they had refused nationalism by attacking English vessels and they had done great damage to the world's capitalist shipping industry. English rulers, Whig and Tory alike, responded by drawing upon and continuing the reforms of the 1690s, hanging sea robbers by the hundreds. Merchants petitioned Parliament, which obliged with deadly new legislation; meanwhile, prime minister Robert Walpole took an active, personal interest in putting an end to piracy. Many historians have claimed that the hangman was not nearly as busy as he might have been in this age of rapidly expanding capital punishments, but the point cannot be proved by pirates. They—and their dreams of Libertalia—were clearly marked for extinction.

The Origins and Subsequent History of Libertalia

We may conclude by considering two questions. From where did Hydrarchy and Libertalia come? And where, once piracy had been formally suppressed, did they go?

First it should be said that the maritime Utopia of the early eighteenth century may well be unique in the annals of piracy (though not, as suggested below, in the annals of the working class). It took a long time for seamen to get, as one man put it, 'the choice in themselves'—that is, the autonomous power to organize the ship as they wanted. Anglo-Atlantic piracy had long served the needs of the state and the merchant community. But there was a long-term tendency for the control of piracy to devolve from the top of society toward the bottom, from the highest functionaries of the state (late sixteenth century), to big merchants (early seventeenth century), to smaller, usually colonial merchants (late seventeenth century), and finally to the common men of the deep (early eighteenth century). When this devolution reached the bottom, when seamen (as pirates) organized a social world apart from the dictates of mercantile and imperial authority and used it to attack merchants' property (as they had begun to do in the 1690s), then those who controlled the state resorted to massive violence, both military (the navy) and penal (the gallows), to eradicate piracy. The social organization of Hydrarchy represented the victory by which the maritime working class had seized control of piracy; the separatism of Libertalia was a necessary response to the state's campaign of terror to reverse that victory.

The sources of the pirates' social order in the early eighteenth century were many, but probably the greatest of them was, as I have argued elsewhere, the experience of work, wages, culture and authority accumulated in the normal, rugged course of maritime life and labour.[5] The pirates' social order cannot be comprehended apart from their previous experiences on merchant, naval or privateering vessels. They transformed harsh discipline into a looser, more libertarian way of running a ship that depended on 'what

---

[5] See Marcus Rediker, *Between the Devil and the Deep Blue Sea: Merchant Seamen, Pirates, and the Anglo-American Maritime World, 1700–1750* (New York: Cambridge University Press, 1987) [Editor].

Punishment the Captain and Majority of the Company shall think fit'. They transformed the realities of chronically meagre rations into near-chronic feasting, an exploitative wage relation into collective risk-bearing, and injury and premature death into concerns for health and security. Their democratic selection of officers stood in stark, telling contrast to the near-dictatorial arrangement of command in the merchant service and Royal Navy. The pirates' social order thus realized tendencies that were both dialectically generated and in turn suppressed in the course of work and life at sea. The culture and experiences of the common seaman constituted the pre-eminent source of Hydrarchy.

A second, closely related source of the pirate social order was the 'Jamaica Discipline' or the 'Law of the Privateers', the body of custom bequeathed to them by the buccaneers who had haunted the Caribbean from roughly 1630 to 1680. This custom boasted a distinctive conception of justice and 'a kind of class consciousness' against 'the great'—shipmasters, shipowners, 'gentlemen adventurers'. It also featured democratic controls on authority and provision for the injured.

* * *

Christopher Hill has suggested the English Revolution as a source of the buccaneers' social order: 'A surprising number of English radicals emigrated to the West Indies either just before or just after 1660', including Ranters, Quakers, Familists, Anabaptists, radical soldiers, and others who 'no doubt carried with them the ideas which had originated in revolutionary England'. A number of buccaneers, we know, went about their work in the 'faded red coats of the New Model Army'. In the New World they insisted upon the democratic election of their officers just as they had done in a revolutionary army on the other side of the Atlantic.[6]

Another intriguing suggestion about the sources of buccaneering culture comes from the late J.S. Bromley. Many French freebooters came, as *engagés*, 'from areas affected by peasant risings against the royal *fisc* and the proliferation of crown agents' in the 1630s. In these regions protesters had shown a capacity for self-

[6] See Hill, "Radical Pirates?" [Editor].

organization, the constitution of 'communes', election of deputies and promulgation of *Ordonnances*, all in the name of 'du Commun peuple'.[7] Such experiences may have informed the social code of the 'Brethren of the Coast' in America.

The buccaneers originated as a kind of multiracial maroon society based on hunting and gathering, formed by unfree labourers (indentured servants and a few slaves) and others who ran from the brutalities of a nascent plantation system. They hunted wild cattle and gathered the king of Spain's gold. They combined the diverse experiences of peasant rebels, demobilized soldiers, dispossessed smallholders, unemployed workers, and others from several nations and cultures, including the Carib and Cuna Indians. Buccaneers knew that their survival in a strange land depended upon their willingness to adapt by drawing on all resources. The 'Custom of the Coast' survived even when high mortality meant that many of the 'Brethren' themselves did not.

How the social and cultural transition from seventeenth-century buccaneer to eighteenth-century pirate worked is, and will probably remain, largely a mystery. But some continuities are clear. Traditions sometimes lived on because a few hearty souls survived the odds against longevity in seafaring work. Some of the old buccaneers themselves served on Jamaican privateers during the War of the Spanish Succession, then took part in the new piracies in peacetime. The Jamaica Discipline and the exploits it made possible also lived on in folktale, song, ballad and memory, not to mention the popular published (and much-translated) accounts of Alexander Exquemelin, Père Labat, and others.

* * *

During the American Revolution, many thousands of captured American seamen were charged as 'pirates' and 'traitors' and herded into British prisons and prison ships, where they quickly organized themselves in the ways of Hydrarchy. According to Jesse Lemisch, these seamen, now autonomous because their officers had

---

[7] J. S. Bromley, "Outlaws at Sea, 1660–1720: Liberty, Equality, and Fraternity among the Caribbean Freebooters," in *History from Below: Studies in Popular Protest and Popular Ideology in Honour of George Rudé*, ed. Frederick Krantz (Montreal: Concordia University, 1985), pp. 301–320 [Editor].

asked to be separated from them, 'governed themselves in accord with abstract notions of liberty, justice, and right' and created a social world characterized by 'egalitarianism', 'collectivism' and commitment to revolutionary ideals.[8] What had functioned as 'articles' among seaman and pirates now became a constitution of sorts, 'a Code of By-Laws for their own regulation and government'. As always they used democratic practices, worked 'to assure the equitable distribution of food and clothing', concerned themselves with questions of health, and established their own distinctive discipline. A captain who looked back at the prison Hydrarchy with considerable surprise remarked that seamen were 'of that class . . . who are not easily controlled, and usually not the most ardent supporters of good order'. What he and others like him failed to understand was that seamen had no trouble supporting an 'order' of their own making.

* * *

Our discussion of Hydrarchy and Libertalia raises questions about the process by which subversive popular ideas and practices are kept alive, underground and over water, for long periods of time. Indeed, the pirates' alternative social order might be seen as a maritime continuation of the traditional peasant Utopia, in England and continental Europe, called 'The Land of Cockaygne'. The dislike of work, the abundance of food, the concern with good health, the levelling of social distinctions and the turning of the world upside down, the redivision of property, the ease and the freedoms—all of the elements of primitive communism that informed the medieval myth were expressed in Libertalia and at least partially realized on the pirate ship.

And yet if Hydrarchy and Libertalia echoed the dreams of Cockaygne in centuries gone by, so did they speak to the future, to the development of mass radical-democratic movements. Hydrarchy and Libertalia may be intermediate popular links between the defeated republicans of the English Revolution and the victorious republicans of the age of revolution more than a century later. The

---

[8] Jesse Lemisch, "Listening to the 'Inarticulate': William Widger's Dream and the Loyalties of American Revolutionary Seamen in British Prisons," *Journal of Social History* 3 (1969–70): 1–29.

relative absence of piracy in the Atlantic between 1750 and 1850 may in the end owe something to the Utopian prospects of an earlier age and the ruthless repression they called forth. But so too might the age of revolution owe something to the Utopian dimensions of earlier popular struggles. Many pirates themselves may have died upon the gallows, defeated, but Hydrarchy and Libertalia had many victories yet to claim.

David Starkey, E. S. van Eyck van Heslinga, and J. A. de Moor, eds., *Pirates and Privateers: New Perspectives on the War on Trade in the Eighteenth and Nineteenth Centuries*. Exeter: University of Exeter Press, 1997, pp. 29–46.

Discourse without Discussion: Representations of Piracy in Colonial Indonesia, 1816–25

JOSEPH N. F. M. À CAMPO

Our understanding of piracy may seem straightforward, but defining it is problematical because the term itself is a social and cultural construct. Concepts of piracy have changed over time and have varied from one region to another. In Western colonial sources indigenous acts of maritime violence are categorically treated as piracy. This confronts modern historiography with many problems of conceptualization, interpretation, and assessment. In this essay Campo uses discourse analysis to help unravel the problem of definitions and perceptions. By comparing differing representations of piracy by Dutch administrators in colonial Indonesia, he shows how piracy was constructed in the confrontation of colonial and indigenous states. In Campo's words piracy is "a concept in development."

In *Almayer's folly*, Joseph Conrad's first novel, Captain Tom Lingard is presented to the reader as ruler of the waves and opponent of pirates. During one of his fights he finds a young girl among the dead pirates in a captured *prahu* (ship). She is prevented by her wounds from defending herself or escaping. He takes her with him, while the *prahu* is set on fire and cast adrift; the orphan, bereft of other relatives and her past, is renamed Nina. He treats her as his daughter, has her brought up in a convent, and eventually gives her away as a bride to his manager Almayer as a seal on their business relationship. Nina regards herself as a child who was captured—not rescued—who resisted in vain; she remembers with great respect 'those brave men she had so much admired and so well helped in their contest with the redoubtable Rajah-Laut'. Although Lingard is at first introduced as an adversary of pirates, the opposition between 'rescue' and 'capture' immediately places him in a critical light as the captor of the child. The introduction of Lingard as a naval hero fits the conventional expectations of the Western reader; at the same time, doubt is raised about the legitimacy of the enforced fatherhood that was presented as well-intended but was by no means disinterested and would eventually fail lamentably. The image of Lingard as both rescuer and captor can be seen as a powerful metaphor for colonialism in general and as a clue to the problem of perspective in the study of the preeminently colonial historical theme of piracy and anti-piracy.

Like the word 'crime' itself and so many other terms in the criminal field, 'piracy' is a term that both describes and passes a (negative) judgement. Research on the history of piracy addresses an object that is *a priori* normatively defined, and is based primarily on sources in which this value judgement goes without saying. The researcher can thus expect many treacherous rocks on his course through the history of piracy, which can only be skirted by looking from more than one angle. A lateral perspective can clarify obstacles and pitfalls in the same way that a floodlight brings out unevenness in a track. That is why an indirect approach has been adopted in the present case: the transformation of the definition of piracy by members of the colonial administration actively involved in native and colonial state formation.

Piracy neither was nor is an unchanging phenomenon; rather, it is a concept in development. The colonial definition evolved under the influence of changing legal concepts, political interests, administrative practices and local conditions. For instance, the British usage of the term piracy to refer to Malay maritime practices in the Straits Settlements was subject to constant modifications of a formula of international law that had been developed in Europe not very long before. Around 1830, for instance, 'piracy' was expanded to include depredations in land territory of the Malay Peninsula along with the corresponding sanctions. To give another example, the British naval officer Sherard Osborn openly admitted that in 1838 the Kedah fleet, which was in revolt against Britain's ally Siam, 'was styled by us as a piratical one'. In that sense, terms like 'piracy', 'banditry' and 'terrorism' can be regarded as labels that one party applies to the actions of the other, even though this is usually done in a less transparent way. This gives the concept of piracy the character of a social construct.

At first glance, this poses an obstacle to a clear view of the factual phenomena that were collectively labelled with the term 'piracy'. However, studying piracy by means of changes in perceptions is an effective way of penetrating biased language usage, and the same is true of propagandist claims to legitimacy based on its suppression. Upon closer inspection, its character as a construct actually makes it possible to describe, compare and deconstruct representations of piracy, thereby throwing the phenomenon itself into clearer relief.

Colonial authors naturally condemned piracy. Moreover, they often wrote with a specific purpose in mind without being bothered by that fact. J. H. P. E. Kniphorst emphasised the scale and destructive character of piracy as a plea to step up the fight against it. J. C. Cornets de Groot, on the other hand, stressed the dedication and effectiveness of the Dutch efforts as a counterweight to less favourable verdicts on them abroad.

The projection of contemporary interests and ambitions also coloured postcolonial, 'Indocentric' historiography from the 1960s onward, in which piracy was presented as one of the expressions of anti-colonial resistance. Exponents of this view include G. J. Resink, Adrian Lapian and Hamid Algadri.[1] More recently, various

---

[1] G. J. Resink, 'The Eastern Archipelago under Joseph Conrad's Western eyes', in his *Indonesia's history between the myths: Essays in legal history and historical theory* (The Hague: W. van Hoeve, 1968), pp. 305–23; Adrian Lapian, 'The sealords of Berau and Mindanao: Two responses to the colonial challenge', *Masyarakat Indonesia* 1, 2 (1974): 143–54; and Hamid Algadri, *Dutch policy against Islam and Indonesians of Arab descent in Indonesia* (Jakarta: LP3ES, 1994. Algardi (p. 62) holds that in the nineteenth century 'any battle at sea against colonial power was called piracy by the Dutch'.

scholars have displayed a tendency to normalise piracy. Carl Trocki and James Warren do so by placing the term within quotation marks, while Richard Leirissa proposes seeing piracy as 'a kind of trade based on theft instead of exchange'.[2] This does imply a certain distance from judgemental language usage, but it brings with it conceptual confusion and a blurring of norms; it therefore offers an insufficient counterweight to a different kind of representation, since what has often happened with raw phenomena from the past (such as banditry in the Wild West or the genocide of Native Americans) occurred with piracy as well. Soon after its sharp reduction in the late 1800s, it was endowed with a romantic sheen in the twentieth century; the entertainment industry in particular created an image of splendour and glory, excitement and heroism.

The current revival of piracy as a phenomenon invites a historical reappraisal. A more down-to-earth approach certainly does not claim that no judgements are made; what it does claim is that the verdict must come not at the beginning of the argument but at the end. * * * Our discussion focuses on the decade between 1816–25 because the views put forward during this relatively short period—the formative stage of the colonial state—provided the format and set the tone for the discourse on piracy during the rest of the nineteenth century.

* * *

Interpretation

That the nineteenth-century definition of piracy was a colonial construct should by no means be taken to suggest that the phenomena collectively referred to as piracy did not really exist. What it does indicate is that the complex of historical phenomena to which it refers was embedded in several layers of meaning which conferred on the term a specific form and content. The study of piracy is almost entirely dependent on one-sided governmental

---

[2] Carl A. Trocki, *Prince of Pirates. The Temenggongs and the development of Johor and Singapore 1784–1885* (Singapore: Singapore University Press, 1979); James F. Warren, *The Sulu zone: The world capitalist economy and the historical imagination* (Amsterdam: VU University Press, 1998), p. 12; Richard Z. Leirissa, 'Changing maritime trade in the Seram Sea', in *State and trade in the Indonesian Archipelago*, ed. G. J. Schurre (Leiden: KITLV Press, 1994), p. 112.

source material, mainly from those branches of the administration responsible for combatting it, which already raises serious problems at even the most simple factual level. In order to gain an impression of the scale of piracy on the basis of the definitions and reports of the time, it is necessary to make corrections and extrapolations for the quantitatively and qualitatively selective perceptions and reports. There are corresponding difficulties when it comes to classification, explanation and interpretation. However, very divergent views have been found within the colonial administration, and comparison of these views can help to redefine concepts for the study of the actual nature, scope, causes, and background of piracy in the Indonesian archipelago in the nineteenth century.

The early discussion of the causes of the development of piracy has led over the years to the emergence of two dominant interpretations of the phenomenon: one more political, the other more economic. The political interpretation is based on the fact that piracy was a means of combat that traditionally had close ties with the relations of power, whereby it could be deployed as an instrument to maintain or challenge a regime. The scale and intensity of piracy in the archipelagos of South-East Asia were a function of the fragmentation and instability of the native political systems. Some administrators ([M. H. W.] Muntinghe,[3] for instance) considered these weaknesses to be inherent; others, like Raffles and Van der Capellen, regarded them as an expression of the general decline brought about by the activities of the VOC. The political interpretation points to the ongoing struggle for power as the dynamic context that produced and maintained piracy, but says little about the question of how it was practised as an economic activity. Piracy as an instrument of power was based on securing and distributing scarce resources—labour, power and commodities—among the leaders and their followers. It was thus an economic phenomenon as well as a political one.

The economic interpretation is based on the assumption that piracy is undertaken for its material advantages, and that piratical enterprises also apply a calculation of costs and benefits. This makes piracy susceptible to analysis in terms of business economics,

[3] Muntinghe's views on piracy are in Doc. 27 [Editor].

and J. L. Anderson has shown that this approach can yield interesting insights which are certainly deserving of empirical testing
and substantiation.[4] The same applies to the analysis of anti-piracy
measures in terms of costs, benefits and risks of protection in the
sense of the controlled exercise of violence; the market form is very
important in this connection. Security is a collective good, which is
why its provision tends towards a natural monopoly. The achievement and legitimation of a monopoly of violence lie precisely at the
core of the processes of state formation, consolidation and decline.
Achievement depends not only on the spatial distribution of costs
and benefits, but also on access to the protection market; and the
key to a monopoly of violence is indeed the control of that access.

The preceding discussion shows that the economic and political
aspects of piracy are generally intertwined, and they certainly were
in the archipelagos of South-East Asia. Given the importance of
violence and legitimation, an economic interpretation therefore
inevitably leads back to the political aspect. That is why it is less
useful to characterise piracy as solely 'economic' or 'political'; both
aspects have to be charted. Forms of piracy can then be distinguished on the basis of differences from both perspectives.

As far as the economic aspect is concerned, a distinction can be
made between parasitical and predatory piracy. The former boils
down to 'creaming off': violently demanding a share in the benefits
of the passing flows of trade, either by robbing vulnerable vessels
or by extortion or more regular levies. The targets are primarily
vessels in the open sea or close to the coasts, and the scale of this
form of piracy depends on the supply. It seems that parasitical
piracy in a more or less regular form was inherent to the native
coastal states. Predatory piracy is essentially "plundering", with
raids undertaken over what are at times very long distances. The
most striking example was based in the sultanate of Sulu, from
where the Illanun organised raids deep into the Indonesian archipelago. Generally speaking, predatory piracy required specially

---

[4] J. L. Anderson, 'Piracy and world history: An economic perspective', *Journal of World
History*, 6 (1995): 175–99; *idem*, 'Piracy in the Eastern Seas, 1750–1850: Some economic im-
plications', in *Pirates and privateers. New perspectives on the war on trade in the eighteenth and nineteenth
centuries*, ed. David Starkey, et al. (Exeter: Exeter University Press, 1997), pp. 87–105.

equipped vessels with a larger crew and heavier weapons than were normal for the parasitical variety. Each form had its own conjuncture; that of parasitical piracy was determined above all by the scale and vulnerability of passing trade flows, and thus by economic developments elsewhere. Predatory piracy, on the other hand, was primarily dependent on the demand for booty—especially slaves—and thus on domestic and regional economic trends in the retail areas. Parasitical piracy tended to exert some strategic restraint, in order to avoid diversion of trade or large-scale retaliation. If predatory piracy showed restraint, it would be for maximising surprise or some other tactical reason.

As for the political aspect of piracy, a distinction can be made between piracy by those wielding power and those in search of it. The powers-that-be in established states could maintain and protect piracy for the advantages it brought in the form of manpower or commodities. They had often come to power through piracy, but once they became established, they usually left the practice of the trade up to enterprising relatives and followers in exchange for a share of the profit. This gave piracy a regular, quasi-legitimate and even businesslike character. Both parasitical and predatory piracy developed cyclically under the protection of established leaders, in so far as the business results were a function of international or regional economic developments. Political conflicts could arise from a recession in trade, but were often its cause, too. Either way, both could lead to 'irregular' piracy by political entrepreneurs ("dissatisfied pirates") who were out for power or sought compensation for the loss of income. The political leaders played an active managerial role in this oppositional piracy and gave the business of piracy a more political colour. Whether they were driven out or left of their own accord, their often opportunistic activities thereby acquired the character of maritime guerrillas. Oppositional piracy therefore developed acyclically or even counter-cyclically.

A combination of the distinction between parasitical and predatory piracy with that between regular and oppositional piracy yields a classification of piracy in four categories. Examples of parasitical piracy under leaders with power were Acheh and Riau-Malay, while the expelled Siakese and Buginese were among those in search

of power. A model of predatory piracy by leaders with power was
offered by the Illanun; the Tobellos represented those in search of
power.

TABLE 1

Typology of Maritime Piracy

		ECONOMIC		
		Parasitic	Predatory	
	Power-holders	Achehnese	Illanun	*cyclical*
		Riau-Malay		
POLITICAL				
	Power-seekers	Siak-Malay,	Tobellorese	*acyclical*
		Buginese		
		supply-driven	*demand-driven*	

Of course, pirates were not so selective as to confine their activities to one of these schematic types. Moreover, parasitical and
predatory piracy became intertwined in some periods and regions,
and regular and oppositional piracy could exist side-by-side or
merge with one another. There is a striking example of this in the
decade under review. The explicitly predatory piracy of the Illanun
expanded after 1780 over virtually the whole archipelago in a relatively short time and linked up in all kinds of places with the native
piracy of the Rayat and Tobellos, so that 'local' piracy became
incorporated intro widespread interregional networks.

Assessment

Combatting piracy was regarded by the colonial administration as
part of the comprehensive programme for the transition from law-
less violence to a legal order, and as the anti-piracy measures
achieved success, they supposedly contributed to the legitimisation
of the colonial state. This somewhat self-complacent vision totally
ignored the fact that the new regime had itself been imposed by
violence in the form of military expeditions, the closing of ports,
the limiting or banning of certain trade, and so on. The postcolonial vision has emphasised precisely this exercise of compulsion by
the colonial government, to the extent that it has even been labelled
as a 'state of violence'. This perspective, which boils down to a sim-

ple reversal of the traditional picture, is equally inadequate because it seriously underestimates the unmistakably important role of violence—legal and illegal—in the native state.

The difference between the native and the colonial states was not the use of violence as such, but its form and function. Native state entrepreneurs needed a supply of slaves from elsewhere to work in the fields and for guard and defence tasks. If they could be obtained directly or indirectly via piracy, that was often a sign of successful state formation. Conversely, slave-exporting districts (Papua, Sumba, Bali, Nias) were characterised by the rudimentary or fragmented formation of power; internal tensions and conflicts were the cause of the taking and selling of slaves, which kept them going. In the experience of the actors themselves, piracy and the slave trade were completely acceptable and even honourable economic activities. The same applies to a certain extent to the many with an interest and involvement in these activities, even among the population from which the victims were taken.

Historical normality may say something about functionality, but it certainly does not say everything about legitimacy. The evaluation of piracy and anti-piracy measures is bound to centre on the question of which aspects of the imposed order were experienced as lawful and beneficial by which sectors of the population. There can be no denying that being kidnapped and sold as a slave was experienced as a personal catastrophe, as is evidenced by scores of testimonies from fugitive slaves. The fact that later on many were obliged to 'get over it' in their new surroundings does not alter the picture. All kinds of groups living on the coasts went in fear of the constant danger of piracy; it was not for nothing that slave-raiders were labelled with terms of invective such as *perompak* [sea pirate] and *penyamun* [robber]. Not only safety, but also prosperity was at stake.

A distinction between the short term and the long term is appropriate here. Piracy was not only a direct assault on a population's meagre possessions, against which it tried to defend itself as best as it could with stone walls and fences made of cacti or palisades. It was above all a brake on population growth and on the achievement of prosperity, because the people often moved away from the coast to the interior and agriculture had to be neglected.

It seems difficult to contradict the claim that the colonial anti-piracy campaigns improved the safety and prosperity of the population in numerous coastal regions even over the long run. A present-day historian, whether from the East or the West, would have to jump over his own shadow to ignore that.

Whatever judgement may be passed in retrospect, a historian describing what happened at the time is constantly required to take into consideration the perspective of that time—including that of the pirates—especially as it appears to linger on. At the start of *Almayer's folly*, Conrad makes it clear that the campaign against the pirates has two sides: while Lingard presents himself as Rajah Laut, Nina continues to dream of 'the glories of the Sultan of Sulu, his great splendour, his power, his great prowess'. As the story takes its course, it becomes increasingly clear that the two are irreconcilable. It is not the choice of one perspective over the other that gives depth and contrast to the narrative of the novel, but rather the way they alternate, interact and mirror one another; something similar applies to the historical discourse on piracy.

Joseph N. F. M. à Campo, "Discourse without Discussion: Representations of Piracy in Colonial Indonesia 1816–25." *Journal of Southeast Asian Studies* 34.2 (June 2003): 199–214.

BIBLIOGRAPHICAL ESSAY

Year after year, new books about pirates appear in print. Unfortunately, many of them add little that is new to our understanding of piracy. Some of the older books remain the best, while several new ones excite the imagination and challenge old stereotypes. This short bibliographical essay mainly introduces readers to the books and articles that I have found most valuable in making sense of the fascinating world of pirates in the age of sail.

Several recent studies dealing with the nature of piracy in a comparative or global perspective are John Anderson's "Piracy and World History: An Economic Perspective on Maritime Predation," *Journal of World History* 6.2 (1995), 175–200; Lawrence Osborne's "A Pirate's Progress," *Lingua Franca* 8.2 (1998): 34–42; and Patricia Risso's "Cross-Cultural Perceptions of Piracy," *Journal of World History* 12.2 (2001): 293–319. Two important collections of essays are David Starkey, J. A. de Moor, and E. S. van Eyck van Heslinga, eds., *Pirates and Privateers: New Perspectives on the War on Trade in the Eighteenth and Nineteenth Centuries* (Exeter: Exeter University Press, 1997); and C. R. Pennell, ed., *Bandits at Sea: A Pirate's Reader* (New York: New York University Press, 2001).

By far the largest number of books and articles are on Western pirates, privateers, and buccaneers. Although not without their critics, anyone seriously interested in understanding the great age of piracy in the West must begin with the classics of Alexandre O. Exquemelin and Captain Charles Johnson, who a number of scholars claim was actually Daniel Defoe. Exquemelin's *The Buccaneers of America* first appeared in Dutch in 1678, and in English translation in 1684. Since that time it has reappeared in various English translations in England and the United States, but a recent translation by Alexis Brown is the most readable (published by Dover Press in 1969). Johnson's (or Defoe's) *A General History of the Pyrates* was published in London in 1724 as a single volume, but because of its

189

tremendous popularity, the author came out with a second volume four years later. It, too, has gone through many printings—and several title changes—and today the best edition is the one edited by Manuel Schonhorn (republished by Dover Press in 1999). Two other useful books, based on primary sources, are George Dow and John Edmonds's *The Pirates of the New England Coast* (first published in 1923; reissued by Dover Press in 1996), and Charles Ellms's *The Pirates Own Book* (first published in 1924; reissued by Dover Press in 1993).

Other important books on the history of Western piracy include Patrick Pringle's *Jolly Roger: The Story of the Great Age of Piracy* (New York: W. W. Norton, 1953), Clive M. Senior's *A Nation of Pirates: English Piracy in Its Heyday* (London: David and Charles, 1976), Frank Sherry's *Raiders and Rebels: The Golden Age of Piracy* (New York: Hearst Marine Books, 1986), and David Cordingly's *Under the Black Flag: The Romance and the Reality of Life among the Pirates* (New York: Random House, 1995). An old but useful study of local piracy along the English coast is David Mathew, "The Cornish and Welsh Pirates in the Reign of Elizabeth," *English Historical Review* 39 (July 1924): 337–348. The book by Janice Thomson, *Mercenaries, Pirates, and Sovereigns* (Princeton: Princeton University Press, 1994), examines piracy in the context of violence, sovereignty, and state building. Peter Earle's recent *The Pirate Wars* (New York: St. Martin's Press, 2003) discusses piracy and its suppression by European states. On Francis Drake, the literature is enormous, though a good place to start is Harry Kelsey's *Sir Francis Drake: The Queen's Pirate* (New Haven: Yale University Press, 1998). For piracy in the Americas, *Pillaging the Empire* (Armonk, N.Y.: M. E. Sharpe, 1998) by Kris E. Lane is an insightful overview. Of the many books on Captain Kidd, the best is by Robert Ritchie, *Captain Kidd and the War against the Pirates* (Cambridge: Harvard University Press, 1986). Another interesting book argues that Kidd was not a pirate but rather, as Richard Zacks's title suggests, a *Pirate Hunter* (New York: Hyperion Press, 2002). Jan Rogoziński's *Honor among Thieves* (Mechanicsburg, Pa.: Stackpole Books, 2000) covers the exploits of Every, Kidd, and other Red Sea pirates. *Villains of All Nations* (Boston: Beacon Press, 2004) by Marcus Rediker is an outstanding scholarly and readable account of the last great epoch of Atlantic piracy in the early eighteenth century. Robert Lee has written an excellent biography entitled *Blackbeard the Pirate* (Winston-Salem, N.C.: John F. Blair, 2002; first published in 1974), and Lindley Butler's *Pirates, Privateers, and Rebel Raiders of the Carolina Coast* (Chapel Hill: University of North Carolina Press, 2000) takes maritime raiding up through the American Civil War.

Several recent writings have broadened our understanding of piracy by addressing issues of gender and sexuality. The history of female pirates is still in its infancy—due in large part to the scarcity of reliable primary sources—but Jo Stanley's *Bold in Her Breeches* (San Francisco: Pandora, 1995) makes good reading that challenges old conceptions. Also useful are several articles in *Iron Men, Wooden Women: Gender and Seafaring in the Atlantic World, 1700–1920* (Baltimore: Johns Hopkins University Press, 1996), edited by Margaret Creighton and Lisa Norling. B. R. Burg's seminal study *Sodomy and the Pirate Tradition* (New York: New York University Press, 1983, 1995) set off a controversy, yet to be resolved, about issues of pirate homosexuality and masculinity. Hans Turley, in *Rum, Sodomy, and the Lash* (New York: New York University Press, 1999), has attempted to answer several questions raised by Burg and others. C. R. Pennell's reader *Bandits at Sea*, includes insightful essays by Marcus Rediker, B. R. Burg, John Appleby, Dian Murray, and Wendy Bracewell on these important topics.

There are not as many books on the Mediterranean corsairs as there are on pirates, and most of the ones in English have been framed in a Western perspective. *Corsairs of Malta and Barbary* (London: Sidgwick and Jackson, 1970) by Peter Earle is reliable and occasionally thought-provoking. A short introduction is Paul Bamford's *The Barbary Pirates: Victims and the Scourge of Christendom* (Minneapolis: University of Minnesota Press, 1972). A recent book by Jacques Heers, *The Barbary Corsairs: Warfare in the Mediterranean, 1480–1580* (London: Greenhill, 2003), covers the early period. On Venice, see Alberto Tenenti's excellent study *Piracy and the Decline of Venice, 1580–1615* (London: Longmans, 1967). More controversial but intellectually stimulating is Peter L. Wilson's *Pirate Utopias: Moorish Corsairs and European Renegadoes*, 2nd rev. ed. (Brooklyn, N.Y.: Autonomedia, 2003). Two valuable articles are Paul Cassar, "The Maltese Corsairs and the Order of St. John of Jerusalem," *Catholic*

Historical Review 46.2 (1960): 137–156, and Stephen Clissold, "Christian Renegades and Barbary Corsairs," *History Today* 26.8 (1976): 508–515. On Christian captives in Barbary, see Ellen Friedman's *Spanish Captives in North Africa in the Early Modern Age* (Madison: University of Wisconsin Press, 1983) as well as the collections of slave narratives in *White Slaves, African Masters: An Anthology of American Barbary Captivity Narratives* (Chicago: University of Chicago Press, 1999), edited by Paul Baepler, and in *Piracy, Slavery, and Redemption: Barbary Captivity Narratives from Early Modern England* (New York: Columbia University Press, 2001), edited by Daniel Vitkus.

As for Asia—including both China and Southeast Asia—there are only a few studies in English on piracy. A short overview of Chinese piracy is in A. D. Blue, "Piracy on the China Coast," *Journal of the Hong Kong Branch of the Royal Asiatic Society* 5 (1965): 69–85. Kwan-wai So's *Japanese Piracy in Ming China during the Sixteenth Century* (East Lansing: Michigan State University Press, 1975), Dian Murray's *Pirates of the South China Coast, 1790–1810* (Stanford: Stanford University Press, 1987), and Robert J. Antony's *Like Froth Floating on the Sea: The World of Pirates and Seafarers in Late Imperial South China* (Berkeley: Institute for East Asian Studies, 2003) cover the great age of Chinese piracy between the sixteenth and early nineteenth centuries. Ralph C. Croizier has examined the role of the pirate-hero in *Koxinga and Chinese Nationalism: History, Myth, and the Hero* (Cambridge, Mass.: Harvard University Press, 1977). An older but still useful book on piracy in post–Opium War China is *British Admirals and Chinese Pirates, 1832–1869* (London: K. Paul, Trench, Trubner & Co., 1940) by Grace Fox.

For Southeast Asia, the best studies are Nicholas Tarling's *Piracy and Politics in the Malay World: A Study of British Imperialism in Nineteenth-Century Southeast Asia* (Singapore: Donald Moore, 1963), Carl A. Trocki's *Prince of Pirates: The Temenggongs and the Development of Johor and Singapore, 1784–1885* (Singapore: Singapore University Press, 1979), and the two books by James Warren, *The Sulu Zone* (Singapore: Singapore University Press, 1981) and *Iranun and Balangingi* (Singapore: Singapore University Press, 2002). Ester Velthoen's "'Wanderers, Robbers and Bad Folk': The Politics of Violence, Protection and Trade in Eastern Sulawesi," in *The Last Stand of*

Asian Autonomies, ed. Anthony Reid (London: Macmillan, 1997), and Ota Atsushi's study *Changes of Regime and Social Dynamics in West Java* (Leiden: Brill, 2006) both add greatly to our understanding of trade and maritime raiding in the East Indies in the early colonial era. Another useful essay that looks at Southeast Asian piracy past and present is Adam Young's "Roots of Contemporary Maritime Piracy in Southeast Asia," in *Piracy in Southeast Asia: Status, Issues, and Responses*, ed. Derek Johnson and Mark Valencia (Singapore: ISEAS, 2005).

Finally, among the many studies of contemporary piracy are Jack A. Gottschalk and Brian P. Flanagan's *Jolly Roger with an Uzi: The Rise and Threat of Modern Piracy* (Annapolis, Md.: Naval Institute Press, 2000), John S. Burnett's *Dangerous Waters: Modern Piracy and Terror on the High Seas* (New York: Dutton, 2002), and Derek Johnson and Mark Valencia, eds., *Piracy in Southeast Asia*. To keep up with the ever-changing world of piracy today, see the International Chamber of Commerce Web site http://www.icc-ccs.org/prc/piracyreport.php.

INDEX